DATE DUE			

Twayne's United States Authors Series

Sylvia E. Bowman, *Editor*

INDIANA UNIVERSITY

Ernest Poole

ERNEST POOLE

By TRUMAN FREDERICK KEEFER

(TUSAS) 110

Twayne Publishers, Inc. :: New York

To

John D. Makosky

of

Western Maryland College

Preface

IN 1915 Ernest Poole, an American journalist, published a novel called *The Harbor*. Almost immediately he became one of the most discussed and most controversial literary figures of the year. Not since Upton Sinclair's *The Jungle* in 1906 had a story about social problems aroused such interest. *The Harbor* became one of the ten best-selling books of the year and was especially popular among the younger intellectuals of college age; it is often said, and there is reason to believe, that this novel profoundly affected the thought of the whole generation that came to maturity during Woodrow Wilson's first term as President. Poole soon solidified his position as an outstanding young writer by winning the newly established Pulitzer Prize in 1917 with *His Family*, a realistic account of life in a middle-class home. Many critics felt that it was an even better book than *The Harbor* and that Poole had proved to be an equal if not the superior of William Dean Howells, the master of the novel of "genteel realism." It is no wonder that Poole's future in literature seemed bright. But within a decade his reputation had faded; and until recently Poole was virtually forgotten, except by social historians, even though he continued writing and publishing books until his death in 1950.

Today, however, there is a revival of interest in Poole, especially among students who have discovered *The Harbor* on an American history reading list and, as a result, now want to read some of his other books. There is, consequently, a need for a complete review of the body of his work; an examination of his social, political, and artistic ideas; a reappraisal of the value of his work; and an investigation into the causes of the rise and fall of his reputation with the critics and the public. The purpose of this study is to satisfy this need and provide a source of information about Poole and his works for the general reader and a foundation for the work of later scholars. Furthermore, it is my hope that this study will rescue from oblivion two substantial novels, *With Eastern Eyes* and *The Destroyer*, works which entitle Poole to an important place among American literary figures.

Because this is a study which concentrates on analysis and criticism of Poole's works, the reader should not expect to find extensive biographical detail; anyone desiring a more detailed treatment of Poole's life, with full footnotes and bibliographies, can refer to my doctoral dissertation, *The Literary Career and Literary Productions of Ernest Poole, American Novelist* (Duke University, 1961).

I wish to acknowledge the contributions which many people have made to my study of Poole. The various librarians, fellow scholars, and correspondents who answered my inquiries are too numerous to list here, but the help of all of them is greatly appreciated. Major sources of information were Mrs. Margaret Ann Poole, the late Otto Mallery, Briscoe R. Smith, and especially William Morris Poole, who was never too busy to answer questions or offer encouragement. I am especially grateful to Professor Clarence Gohdes of Duke University, the advisor of my doctoral dissertation on Poole. Lastly, I wish to thank two friends—George Winter, whose uncompromising views on style inspired many revisions and improvements, and Mrs. Janet Guenther, without whose assistance as typist and critic this book could not have been completed.

T. F. KEEFER

Middletown, Ohio, 1966

Contents

Chronology

1880   Ernest Cook Poole born on January 23 in Chicago, fifth
       of seven children, second son of Abram Poole, well-to-do
       stockbroker, and Mary Howe Poole, daughter of prom-
       inent Chicago family.

1898- Attended Princeton. A slow start academically in first two
1902   years; earned A's from Woodrow Wilson in history and
       political science; became interested in the forces shaping
       the modern world. Decided to become writer.

1902- In September moved to University Settlement House,
1904   Lower East Side, New York City; became social worker
       as means of collecting fresh literary material. Drifted into
       "muckraking," produced articles on child labor, tubercu-
       losis-producing slums, sweat-shop conditions, rent-gougers.

1904   In June, returned to Chicago, wrote articles on Teamsters
       Union; in July, reported on six-week strike in stockyards;
       became public relations man for strikers. Death of mother,
       Mary Howe Poole.

1904- In December, interviewed Russian revolutionary, Kath-
1905   arine Breshkovsky. After Winter Palace massacre, secured
       commission from *Outlook* to report 1905 revolution.
       Visited Russia; articles on country brought him recogni-
       tion as correspondent.

1905- Became well-known as writer of short fiction about life
1911   of immigrant in America; wrote unsuccessful first novel,
       The Voice of the Street (1906). Married Chicago debu-
       tante, Margaret Winterbotham, in February, 1907; moved
       to Greenwich Village and continued career as prominent
       and prolific journalist. Son, William Morris, born in
       February, 1908. Joined moderate wing of Socialist Party
       in 1908 at urging of Morris Hillquit; joined staff of *New
       York Call*. Composed a dozen plays, saw three produced
       with modest success.

1912- Inspired by textile strikes led by Industrial Workers of
1914 the World, composed over a two-year period his most
famous work, *The Harbor* (1915). Immediately became
famous and controversial novelist. In November, 1912,
second son, Nicholas, born.

1914- Spent November, December, January (1914-1915) as war
1917 correspondent inside Germany and on German front lines.
Decided to devote career to novel writing, composed *His
Family*; won in 1917 first Pulitzer Prize ever awarded a
novel. Wrote *His Second Wife*. Daughter Betsy Ann born
in 1916.

1917- On American entry into World War 1 withdrew from
1920 pacifistic Socialist Party; served as propagandist on George
Creel's Committee on Public Information. In July, visited
Russia to observe problems of Kerensky Republic; produced series of articles urging American aid (collected as
The Dark People in 1918) and describing his trip (collected as *The Village: Russian Impressions* in 1918). After
Armistice wrote *Blind* to express his disillusionment with
the "war to end war" and the Red Scare.

1921 Published *Beggars' Gold,* novelette.

1922 Published *Millions*.

1923 Published *Danger*. Visited Fascist Italy as correspondent,
wrote articles warning of this new menace.

1924 Published *The Avalanche*.

1925 Published *The Hunter's Moon*. Issued collection of
Russian folktales and stories of psychic phenomena, *The
Little Dark Man*. Reviewers began to describe Poole as
"written out."

1926 Reported on critical sessions of League of Nations in
Geneva. Found easy market for numerous short works in
magazines. Published *With Eastern Eyes*.

1927 Published *Silent Storms,* his last popular success in fiction.

1929 Published long magazine story on capitalist Captain
Dollar. In the crash lost much of his inherited wealth.

1930 Published *The Car of Croesus,* a reworking of magazine
stories.

1931   Published *The Destroyer*. Began publishing articles on the Depression; worked to raise funds to alleviate suffering.

1932   Produced articles and book (*Nurses on Horseback*) to raise funds for Frontier Nursing Service in Kentucky.

1933   Expressed views on the Depression in *Great Winds*.

1934   Published *One of Us*.

1936   Macmillan Company rejected *The House That Grew Young* as unsaleable, requested "another *Harbor*"; manuscript also rejected by Houghton-Mifflin. Abandoned writing novels for twelve years.

1937   Toured Europe as correspondent. Reported again on Fascist regime in Italy; described economic crisis in France and coronation of George VI in England.

1938   Began work on *The Bridge*, autobiography and summation of the major events of his time. Book sold 2,369 copies.

1940-   Two trips to England when commissioned by *Redbook* to
1941   cover Battle of Britain and war effort. After Pearl Harbor, volunteered for service in Office of War Information but was rejected.

1942   Began work on *Giants Gone: The Men Who Made Chicago* (1943).

1943-   At request of Doubleday editor Howard Cady began re-
1946   search for book on New Hampshire, Poole's summer home and retreat since before World War I. Completed after four years in 1946 as *The Great White Hills of New Hampshire*.

1947-   Wrote *The Nancy Flyer* (March, 1948). Suffered slight
1949   stroke early in 1948; then a major one in autumn as result of overwork on revisions.

1950   After over a year of increasing paralysis and mental disability died on January 10, 1950.

Ernest Poole

CHAPTER 1

Foreshadowings

I *Family Background*

ERNEST POOLE, who was born in his father's mansion in Chicago in 1880, later became the author of the most famous socialist novel of his time and spent much of his adult life in attacking the class into which he had been born. The obvious question is, why did his life follow this unlikely course? The answer lies to a great extent in his essentially middle-class background and in the traits which he acquired directly from his parents.[1]

Poole's conception of his place in American society was molded by the fact that his family did not belong to an aristocracy of wealth and cultivation. He could trace its lineage back eight generations to a Dutchman named Vanderpoel, who had settled in New York when it was still ruled by his countrymen; but none of the descendants had been outstanding in public life or the arts. Instead, they were ordinary "solid citizens" whose industry, thrift, and hard-headed practicality brought them prosperous farms, substantial businesses, and some prominence in their own small communities. Not until after the Civil War did one of them, Poole's father, Abram, leave the farm and acquire a fortune; yet even he never thought of himself as being one of the upper classes; instead, he took pride in being an ordinary, honest, hard-working, small-town American. His son, who unconsciously absorbed his parent's attitude, never felt that he was different from the countless average Americans he would find suffering from social injustice. It is not surprising, therefore, that Poole devoted many years to defending their claim to equality.

But his middle-class background also tended to pull him in the opposite direction: generations of the Poole family had passed down the tradition that a man's primary obligation was to provide well for his family and his children's future. Ernest Poole sometimes found it difficult to reconcile this view with his responsibility to society, and it is not unusual to find characters in his novels facing the same dilemma.

Many of Abram Poole's traits reappeared in his son. One example was his generosity toward the unfortunate to whom his charity was often unwisely extravagant. From his father, the energetic and determined businessman who made and lost three fortunes in ten years before he secured a fourth, Poole acquired the capacity for hard work and the stubborn refusal to quit that often drove him to mental and physical collapse; the picture he later drew of a fictional exhausted businessman was based on memories of his father. From his father, too, came the son's esthetic leanings. Abram Poole had an artistic streak; he was an amateur violinist, he loved plays and concerts, he collected rare and beautiful violins, and he encouraged his children to develop similar interests. He was a man who loved to read Dickens and Thackeray aloud and to tell stories of real life experiences to his friends. Because of these characteristics, Abram Poole was admirably suited to be the father of a son whose career was to be storytelling.

Ernest Poole's mother, Mary Howe Poole, was the dominant influence in his life. She came from a family of long-established wealth and respectability, one that had been prominent for years when her husband-to-be first came to Chicago with nearly empty pockets. Reared in a strict Presbyterian household, she practiced quietly the self-discipline and the ethical code which had been taught her. She had remarkably little self-righteousness and intolerance in her attitudes; consequently, she was loved for her pleasantness, her generosity, her serene and cheerful view of life, and her unending sympathy and understanding. Reared by her in a home filled with love and security, Poole acquired naturally a sane, optimistic, and happy view of life as well as a large share of her emotional stability. Following his mother's example, he was nearly always tolerant of others' points of view and generous toward the needy; therefore, like her, he had many friends and got along well with people in spite of his shyness. In later years when he became an agnostic he never abandoned the ethical and moral concepts learned in his childhood, and it may be argued that his interest in reform movements and socialism was simply an extension of private Christian ethics into the broader area of public morality. All things considered, it is not surprising that Poole eventually married a woman much like his mother and that the two of them are reflected in many of the women characters in his novels.

It is obvious that most of the characteristics of Poole as an adult were inherited or acquired from his family background. It is less easy to find an explanation of other qualities of this man. There is, for example, no apparent reason in his ancestry or upbringing for the shyness and sense of personal inadequacy that always made him feel he was an outsider. Nor is it clear how eight generations of unexcitable bourgeoisie could produce a man with the sensitivity, imagination, and intuitive understanding of other people so essential to the creation of literary works.

II *Childhood and Adolescence*

The first five years of Poole's life were happy, safe, and secure; the next twelve were filled with experiences, often painful, that shaped his character, his views on life, and his choice of a career. The first formative incident occurred shortly after he was six and began attending the University School for Boys. On the first declamation day in public speaking class he was overcome by stage fright, forgot his speech, and was driven to tears of shame and frustration by the laughter of other students. Eventually, he managed to stumble through such recitations, but his first experience haunted him throughout life; as an adult, he consistently refused to make speeches of any kind and spoke with assurance and ease only in small gatherings of friends.

Other happenings of an unpleasant nature took place at Lake Forest, where the Pooles spent their summers. One unforgettable event was the accidental drowning of a playmate, which brought to young Poole the knowledge and fear of death. The other incident occurred at an outing for poor boys from the Half Orphan Asylum in the city: one of the orphans, after seeing the Pooles' home and possessions, blurted out, "Jesus Christ, but it's hell to be poor!" For the first time Poole realized that all people did not have a life as fortunate as his. He later described this discovery as marking the beginning of his social consciousness and his career as a social reformer.

Later, when he was ten or eleven, he learned even more about life when he joined a gang of boys who played games in the city dumps and around the lumber yards on the lake front. These good friends, who were not rich men's sons, taught him a respect for people regardless of class that later helped him win the confidence of the slum dwellers whom he studied as material for his books. Furthermore, this companionship helps explain why his sympathies for the underprivileged were always easily aroused. Many of Poole's experiences were recalled twenty-five years later when he put them into his novel, *The Harbor*. One that was extremely disturbing took place about 1892; after discovering Poole's complete ignorance concerning sex, a member of his gang took him into the red-light district, "where from a lighted window a naked fat woman beckoned and smiled." As Poole stared at her, his guide explained to him in crude terms how he had been conceived and born. This sudden introduction to the "facts of life" left the boy shocked and filled with disgust for sex and women. When his mother discovered what had happened, she gave him a book which explained human reproduction in more refined terms and thereby enabled him to understand what he had seen and to gain some sense of proportion. Nevertheless, the shocking memory never left him; it probably inhibited his relationships with women as it did those of his character, Billy, to whom the same thing happened in *The Harbor*.

During adolescence, Poole developed interests that affected his later career. For a time he did work on the school paper. He attended the theater frequently and acquired a passion for the stage which ultimately led to his unsuccessful attempts to be a playwright. Music, however, was the subject that interested him most. He dreamed of becoming a famous composer or performer, and as early as 1892 he began to take violin lessons. He showed such diligence and promise that his parents permitted him to postpone college for a year while he continued with the violin and studied harmony and composition. At last, though, it became clear to him that no amount of practice would make him a virtuoso and that he lacked the ability to write music that would express his emotions. Simultaneously, the thought of a literary career began to appeal to him more and more, especially since storytelling had fascinated him from childhood. By the fall of

1898 he had definitely given up his ambition to become a professional musician. Yet his years of hard work were not in vain: he had learned how to work hard in the pursuit of a goal; and, equally important, as he said later, his study of music had trained his ear to be sensitive to the rhythms and accents of speech and thus greatly aided him in composing dialogue and capturing dialect.

In 1893 the Chicago World's Fair (the "White City") opened its gates to the world, and among those profoundly impressed by it was young Ernest Poole. The exposition presented the best work done by American art and science, and it symbolized the advances men hoped to make in the twentieth century when, it was predicted confidently, scientific planning would bring beauty and order to the ugly, inefficient metropolitan areas of the world and when automatic machines would free mankind from soul-crippling toil. That vision of the future remained with Poole long after the fair closed, and probably his career as a social reformer owed much of its fervor to that belief in progress which the "White City" fostered.

By 1898 the process of growing up had left Poole with a number of permanent scars, but it had also implanted ideals that would guide his life. Most important, maturation had brought out the traits which most characterized him as an adult—a tendency to be optimistic, a capacity for self-directed and unrelenting hard work, and the ability to accept and make the best of unpleasant truths. He was not equipped to win all his battles with life, and would certainly lose many; but it was not likely that the experience would destroy him.

III *College Days*

Poole's four years at Princeton were marked by a series of stinging personal failures and disappointments, by his first attempts to learn the craft of writing, and by his discovery—almost accidentally—of the subject matter that would dominate much of his later work. It was a period of disillusionment, false starts, and, finally, significant progress toward his chosen career.

Poole always spoke of his stay at Princeton with uncharacteristic bitterness. He was unsparing in his criticism of the many outdated courses and incompetent professors, and he often declared that his education was worthless. There may have been considerable truth in his account of the school's academic weaknesses, but he actually learned much more than he admitted; he was, in fact, graduated *cum laude* with special honors in history and politics. The truth is that his attacks owe their virulence to his resentment of something entirely different—a series of humiliating rebuffs handed him by his classmates, defeats which soured his attitude toward Princeton. As a freshman he competed for a position on the editorial staff of the daily paper, the *Princetonian*, and for membership in the Mandolin Club; in both cases he was not elected.[2] As a sophomore, Poole, who had only a few close friends, was blackballed by the fraternity he had chosen and was finally grudgingly accepted only when his roommate, Otto Mallery, refused to join without him. In his third and fourth years Poole participated in a number of extracurricular activities, but he never won a position of leadership; as a result, his classmates at graduation voted him their "most useless man." The epithet was, of course, the crowning indignity. Poole was so deeply hurt that this experience doubtless distorted his view of his achievement at Princeton.

One worthwhile accomplishment of his college days was his first serious attempts at learning to write. For a while he served as a reporter for the *Princetonian*, but when he found himself making no progress, he began working diligently on his own. He received no encouragement from the editors of campus publications until the fall of his sophomore year, when one of his compositions appeared in the *Nassau Literary Magazine*.[3]

Poole's story, "An Author's Predicament," is of more than passing interest because of what it shows of the writer's proficiency—and his weaknesses—in 1899. The plot, which concerns the efforts of a young author to convince his fiancée that she had not overheard a proposal of marriage to a rival but, rather, a discussion of a love scene in the book he is writing, is, at best, a mildly amusing example of old-fashioned undergraduate humor; but it does have directness and clarity. The hero and the two girls display no more depth than the line drawings in an old college annual; the trusty friend, a homely misfit inclined to Byronic melancholy yet shrewd enough to solve the predicament, is more clearly realized but owes his origin to contemporary literary models. The style, the most successful aspect of the story, shows care and polishing; the dialogue is, in general, acceptable but not brilliant. Furthermore, the handling of the technical problems involved in the first half of the narrative, which is told entirely in a series of letters, is surprisingly skillful. One should observe, however, that Poole may have been imitating the example set by Thomas Bailey Aldrich in his widely read "Marjorie Daw" (1873); yet unlike Aldrich and with remarkable disdain for consistency in point of view, he told the rest of the story in the third person. It is not likely that he abandoned the example of his model because his inventiveness failed; he simply was not concerned with consistency, for many of his most carefully constructed works in later years are marred by the same fault. In spite of its flaws, "An Author's Predicament" deserves the adjective "promising."

The story has further interest because the literary theories, practices, and problems of the fictional author bear a remarkable resemblance to those of Poole as a mature writer. The hero, for example, considers himself a "realist," a term which to him means one who relies heavily on information garnered from real life rather than from the imagination. As the story opens, he is asking a female friend how she would react to a certain situation which he plans to use in a work of fiction. Ernest Poole, as will be seen, throughout his career frequently borrowed material from his own experiences and those of others. Another facet of the writer's art—revision—is mentioned by the fictional novelist; he describes how he spent a whole night locked in his room, writing and revising until the composition was free of flaws, doing the "hardest work" he had ever attempted. Again there is a resemblance to Poole, the professional writer, who often rewrote a novel as many as five or six times.

The hero also faces a problem which repeatedly returned to plague Poole in later years—the character who develops traits of which the author is not aware and thus makes the outcome of the story unbelievable and the action unsatisfactorily motivated; but Poole's author luckily discovers in time that his plot requires a more forceful heroine and makes the necessary changes. Poole on occasion was less perceptive but was aware, even in 1899, that such a problem could occur. It seems almost certain that "An Author's Predicament" gives an accurate picture of Poole at the beginning of his writing career; at the very least, it reveals his intimate acquaintance with the procedures and pitfalls of actual composition of fiction; for this reason one is surprised to find in the story imitation of literary models instead of life and far too little attention to characterization. Clearly, the young author preached better than he practiced.

His success as a campus writer was short-lived; "An Author's Predicament" remained his only published work. One of his plays was described as "promising" by a professor, but it never was considered worthy of production. He also submitted two librettos to the Triangle Club, the musical comedy group of the school; both of these efforts were rejected. Poole's disappointment must have been immense, yet (and this reaction was typical of him) his determination to go on writing was only strengthened by these new setbacks. He began devising new methods of learning his chosen craft.[4]

Reading was an important part in this preparation. He spent much of his free time browsing and reading in the Princeton library. He discovered Tolstoy and *War and Peace,* which he always considered the greatest novel ever written. He also liked *Anna Karenina* and the stories about the Cossacks. There was also Turgenev; Poole became fond of *Fathers and Sons, Virgin Soil,* and *A Sportsman's Sketches*—indeed, of everything that master had written. It was only fitting that in a few years he would see firsthand the scenes and peoples of rural Russia which *A Sportman's Sketches* had portrayed so vividly. Other favorites were Maupassant, O. Henry, Balzac, Kipling, and Stevenson.

Poole did not make the mistake of believing that one could learn to write only by reading. He knew that writing and rewriting were essential to his goal. He now began to imitate the style and methods of the authors whom he admired, studying them closely to see how they had solved the technical aspects of prose which sometimes baffled him. His model for brevity and clarity was Stevenson; he patterned his style after that of Turgenev, who exemplified quiet beauty and strength; he analyzed O. Henry and Maupassant because they excelled in organization and ability to construct plots.

Nevertheless, after all this preparation and effort he still found himself unable to produce acceptable stories. There seem to be two main reasons for this failure. First, he was not one of those naturally gifted writers to whom words come easily. Second, he had not yet found a subject that would be peculiarly his own and would so possess him that all his potential as a writer would be realized. All he had was the desire to become an author and the willingness to work at the task. Hence, his earliest writings were bloodless imitations of the authors he had read.

Fortunately for his career as a novelist, Poole found, during his last two years in college, material he was to use for most of his life—the strange new forces that were reshaping America and the world. As it happened, this interest in current events grew out of his reading in Tolstoy and Turgenev of the social upheavals in Russia. Soon he began to wonder whether similar changes were taking place in his own country. He learned some of the answers from Woodrow Wilson, who gave brilliant lectures on contemporary political issues to classes often numbering four hundred and who constantly urged students to take an active part in reforming America's political institutions and abolishing its social evils.[5] Stimulated by what he heard, Poole began to read everything he could find about social trends and the forces which were already changing the world in which he had been born. The book which he said changed the course of his life was Jacob Riis's *How the Other Half Lives* (1890), which told in simple form the story of the slums of New York. All of his latent sympathies for the underdog were aroused by Riis's book. There, in the tenements, lay the challenge to young men that Wilson had described. But—and this fact, rather than social reform, seems to have been uppermost in Poole's mind—the slums also appeared to him a virtually untouched field of material awaiting the first writer to discover its worth. In the streets of New York he would be able to find countless ideas for stories and characters as well as a romantic and exotic background formed by the mélange of immigrants from a dozen nations. There, surely, he would learn to write, he told himself; and when he left the Princeton campus after his graduation in June of 1902, he was filled with renewed confidence in his future.

CHAPTER 2

From Journalism to Literature
via Socialism

I *The Muckraker*

IN THE FALL OF 1902 Ernest Poole moved into the University Settlement House on New York City's Lower East Side and began working as a resident social worker under the direction of Robert Hunter. The job and location were ideally suited to his purpose—the observation of immigrant life and the collection of material that could be used as a basis for the fiction he hoped to write and publish. He had no intention of becoming a reformer; apparently he really believed that the experience of living intimately with poverty and social injustice would not affect his plans. He was wrong; a generation of young people intent on social reform was one of the chief products of the settlement houses, and nearly all of Poole's future writing reflected his concern for the victims of social and economic repression.

He was quickly drawn into the reform movement when Hunter asked him to prepare for the New York Child Labor Committee a report on child labor in the city streets. Because he was able to win the confidence of the newsboys, bootblacks, and messenger boys with whom he talked, Poole soon assembled an abundance of shocking material. He was able to refute with ease the popular contention that work was good for the boys, that it built character and produced worthy citizens. Instead, because of irregular hours of sleeping and eating, lack of schooling, and absence of parental guidance in an environment dominated by crime and vice, the boys were stunted physically, intellectually, and morally, and most of them were soon claimed by jails, hospitals, and morgues. Poole's findings were published early in 1903 in pamphlet form and in several magazines.[1] Thus his first published works were not fiction, as he had planned, but were, instead, factual contributions to the literature of exposure. They were an appropriate beginning since his novel *The Harbor* (1915) is often described as the best literary work to come out of that genre and the muckraking movement.

In these early days of his career, writing proved to be a difficult art for the young man to master in spite of the many hours he spent at his desk. Help and advice came from his new acquaintances at the settlement house. William English Walling taught him to listen closely to his subjects, and Leroy Scott helped him select and organize his materials. Lincoln Steffens urged him to work for content and emotion rather than niceties of style—to put down on paper raw "chunks of life." Ray Stannard Baker, who was responsible for Poole's lifelong habit of taking notes, taught him how to observe closely and select the significant details which would bring a page to life. Baker also told Poole that the best way to give focus to his work was to pick out a typical American of his acquaintance and write as though he were speaking to him. Although the assistance and encouragement of his colleagues enabled him to sell his factual articles, it was of no help in selling his fiction, which was consistently rejected by editors.

His friends at the settlement house tried hard to convert him to a full-time career as reformer and social worker. Even though he was constantly exposed to their ideas, he found Marxist and socialist dogma dull and did not wish to substitute another rigid system of belief for the Presbyterianism he had recently escaped. Furthermore, he had come to New York to learn to write: social work was a means to an end. He intended to write fiction, not propaganda.

In the spring of 1903, however, he became involved in the fight against tuberculosis in the slums and for a time nearly abandoned his goal. The Committee on the Prevention of Tuberculosis asked him to collect human interest stories that could be used to make the public aware of the suffering and loss of life caused by disease-producing slum conditions. Poole gained access to the squalid, crowded flats where victims of the White Plague lay coughing out their lungs. There was no shortage of horrifying case histories: one block had 265 recorded fatalities in nine years. The pamphlet *The Plague in its Stronghold* and two magazine articles[2] show how well Poole had carried out his assignment; even today the reader is shocked, sickened, and overwhelmed with pity and outrage. But for the young man the writing was not enough; he became obsessed with the need to effect change at once. He used his own money to secure help for some of the victims, but the job was too large for any individual. The only answer lay in immediate action by an aroused public through state legislation. All during the summer and into the fall he worked frantically toward this goal, even testifying before an investigating committee in Albany. But in the end no action was taken because the politicians were afraid to offend the influential owners of the tenements.

Because he had been so emotionally involved in the fight, the defeat was a bitter experience. There was now nothing more which he could do to help those living in the slums, and he at last saw clearly the indifference of the wealthy and was forced to acknowledge their power to stop even the best-planned and most desperately needed reforms. Eventually he would have to accept the contention of his settlement friends that only in a socialist state could the corrupting power of wealth be restrained and true reform accomplished. The anger produced by this first encounter with corrupt politicians never left him, and he never completely gave up writing and working in support of reforms— even in his later years when he became a conservative and a little ashamed of his days as a muckraker.

Although Poole indicated in his life story, *The Bridge*, that he abandoned reform after the state's failure to act on housing laws, the fact is that he continued his career as a muckraker. Articles on tuberculosis appeared as late as April, 1904, and there were others on voting violations in the Bowery; the wages, hours, and working conditions in sweatshops and garment factories; and rent-gouging in the tenements. Among his recommendations were a higher income for the lower classes to give them an economic stake in the elections, public support of unions, and low cost public housing.[3]

At last, in the early months of 1904, he achieved his original goal, the one he had when he came to the Lower East Side: two short stories were accepted by John Cosgrave of *Everybody's*

Magazine. In these stories he solved the problem of giving reality to his fiction by a simple expedient—the lavish use of characters and incidents from real life, a practice he was to follow even later when he was a well-known novelist. The first of these stories, "Dutch and the Skinner," contrasts two very dissimilar adolescent boys of the street who strike up a friendship based on their complementary qualities. The slow-witted but reliable Dutch and the quick-witted, restless, spendthrift Skinner, who gambles away their savings in his search for easy money, were based on street boys Poole had actually met. The characters are as real as life, the dialogue is authentic, and there is no overt social message. The second of the stories, "A Slow Man," deals with the attempt of a forty-year-old immigrant, who is nearly blind from working in a garment factory, to learn to read English so that he may obtain a new position as a janitor. The social message is implicit in the story: the newcomer's vision of the promise of America should not be extinguished by sweatshops and grinding poverty.[4]

By June, 1904, he had left the settlement house; and, caught up in other activities and ventures, he did not return. But his residence there had worked profound changes. His exposure to the realities of social injustice and to the ideas of his liberal friends had made him a reformer for the rest of his life—the propagandist he had not wanted to be. Yet, as a writer, he could claim a moderate success. He had begun to learn his craft; he had caught the attention of magazine editors who would thereafter solicit work from him; and he had placed ten competent factual articles and two short stories of worth. And, of equal importance, he had absorbed much material he was to use later in short stories and in such novels as *The Voice of the Street*, *The Harbor*, and *Blind*.

II *Chicago's Unions*

During the summer and fall of 1904 Poole became deeply involved in the struggles of organized labor in Chicago and in the process took another step toward socialism and to the later writing of *The Harbor*, which grew in part out of the events of this year. His first connection with the Chicago unions was the result of a commission by *World Today*, a liberal magazine, to report on recent internal struggles in the powerful International Brotherhood of Teamsters. "How a Labor Machine Held up Chicago" presents in detail one of the early attempts of racketeers to use the power of a strong union to obtain personal power and wealth. In this case the union ousted its corrupt leadership and, Poole felt, demonstrated the integrity and honesty of the labor movement. He also observed that the continued existence of a union that could force its will on even die-hard capitalists like Marshall Field was a significant social development, a demonstration of the emergence of the class struggle predicted by the Marxists. When the Teamsters Union began to use its power to support strikes by other relatively defenseless unions, it was not difficult to foresee a proletarian revolution growing out of a united labor front. Poole later used such a turn of events as the central action of *The Harbor*.[5]

A second article, "The Disappearing Public," gave further support to his thesis that class warfare was imminent. No longer, he argued, was there a "public" outside the struggle between labor and capital. Even white-collar groups were being forced into unions to obtain a living wage, and professional groups with vested interests allied themselves with the employer class who were working to prevent any reforms and to stamp out the unions. The outcome, Poole felt, would be a civil war along class lines.[6]

If Poole wondered which side he would choose, he found the answer in July and August when he and William Hard were sent by *Outlook* to report on a major nine-city strike by the Amalgamated Meat Cutters and Butcher Workmen. Twenty thousand men left their jobs in the Chicago stockyards when the meat-packers refused to pay non-union, unskilled workers a minimum of less than nineteen cents an hour—hardly a living wage. The union, then, had little to gain for itself and was fighting to protect helpless fellow workers. The joint report by Poole and Hard was completely sympathetic to the workers. The issue, they said, was whether wages should be based on the needs of the workers, who already lived in filth and poverty, or on the size of the available labor pool. They called for government intervention and the establishment of a board of arbitration that would work out a salary scale based on the cost of living.[7]

During his six weeks' stay in Packingtown, Poole wrote additional pieces for magazines and did all in his power to assist the workers. Impressed by the attempts of union leader Michael Donnelly to prevent violence, he volunteered to act as press agent for the union and even placed a pro-union article in the *Independent*. His efforts were in vain, however, because the government did not intervene. The strike and the union were starved out of existence, and not even Poole's claim of a moral victory in a selfless cause was much compensation for two months of suffering by the families of the union members.[8]

The strike made a deep and lasting impression on him. Memories of the events of the summer of 1904 and the intimate knowledge he had gained of the workings of unions enabled him to present in *The Harbor* pictures of labor strife that have seldom been equaled in vividness and accuracy. In it, for example, was a dramatic scene he had actually watched—the leader addressing ten thousand strikers at a great open-air meeting. Also in *The Harbor* appeared the character Jim Marsh, whose portrait owed much to Michael Donnelly.[9] The idealism of the strikers had convinced Poole of the ability of the people to rise above themselves and to work together for a common cause. Simultaneously, the callousness of the packers had brought him to the conclusion that only socialism or governmental regulation would bring an end to economic exploitation and social injustice. He did not formally join the Socialist Party until several years later, but henceforth he gave his support to many of its programs.

The defeats and hurts which Poole had received in the world had been painful, but a sharper and more personal grief remained to be undergone. His mother died of cancer in the winter of 1904. Her death was perhaps the greatest personal loss ever sustained by Poole, for there had been a strong bond of affection between them. Moreover, she had symbolized to him the world of his childhood, the safe and settled world where kindliness, order, and love prevailed, where unwelcome change never intruded. Perhaps for the first time in his life he experienced the feeling of being alone and defenseless in an unfriendly cosmos. In the years that followed, her influence on him continued, and, either consciously or unconsciously, he modeled some of the women characters in his novels on Mary Howe Poole; it is apparently no coincidence that a number of them also die of cancer at the end of virtuous lives.

III *Russia*

One of the most exciting and memorable experiences of Poole's life was his trip to Russia in 1905 as a correspondent for *Outlook*. Only twenty-five and with barely two years of experience as a journalist, with no knowledge of Russian and protected against the dangers of a police-state by little more than a sublime confidence in his own invulnerability, he lived and traveled for three months inside Russia, interviewed hundreds of people, and produced a series of articles whose authenticity and power made him one of the most widely known correspondents of the time.

The now-famous Winter Palace massacre on January 22, 1905, when troops killed five hundred peaceful petitioners, was the event that made the trip to Russia possible. Poole persuaded the editors of *Outlook* that a revolution was now certain and asked that he be sent to report it as it began. They agreed to do so because he had performed well as a writer during the stockyards strike; and, furthermore, his acquaintance with such exiles as Katharine Breshkovsky, whom he had interviewed and made a national celebrity,[10] provided him with contacts in Russia that another correspondent would not find readily. Thus, on January 28, posing as the representative of an American firm that was considering the opening of a branch in St. Petersburg, he left for Europe—carrying money and secret messages for the revolutionists.

His investigation, conducted with the help of a Russian interpreter named Tarasov, was both intensive and extensive. For several weeks Poole talked with socialists, student groups, and factory workers in St. Petersburg and then smuggled a report of his first impressions out to his publisher. Afterwards he spent four days in peasant villages studying attempts by agitators to gain the support of the rural masses, without whose backing the revolution would fail. Two weeks in Moscow sightseeing and collecting information on the local labor movement were followed by a tour of Ukrainian villages and industrial cities, where bloody suppression of earlier revolts had wiped out all resistance to the Czar. The climax of the trip was an extended visit to the Caucasus, where hardy tribesmen and Georgian nationalists were waging guerilla warfare in the mountains while the labor movement in the cities staged successful general strikes. When he at last entrained for London in March, he had captured on film, in notes, and in his remarkably retentive mind the most deeply stirring story of his time.

During the remainder of the spring of 1905, while living in London and Paris, Poole painstakingly shaped his material into fourteen magazine articles. As he had done in his earlier work, he sprinkled his text with anecdotes to illustrate his main points. Whenever possible, he let his sources tell their own stories by using lengthy literal transcripts of their conversations, a method that he had employed successfully in his story on Katharine Breshkovsky.

Poole never surpassed his articles for *Outlook*. Fifty years later his wife pointed to the first one in the series as the best short piece he had ever done,[11] and these writings firmly established his reputation as a correspondent. Even today they make stimulating reading because his reporting and analysis are surprisingly accurate (no small accomplishment considering the handicaps imposed by the short duration of the stay, the language barrier, and the official censorship). Equally important, his descriptions capture the scenes, the atmosphere, and the people of Russia with such vividness that one does not need to look at the accompanying photographs.

The Russian expedition was an invaluable experience. It brought out a latent talent as a writer, inspired him to produce some of his best magazine pieces, and thus gained him wide recognition as a journalist. It also provided him with an abundance of material which eventually was employed in a score of short pieces and, in later years, in the novels *The Harbor*, *Blind*, *With Eastern Eyes*, and *The Car of Croesus*. It is no wonder that he always looked back with pleasure to those stirring days when Russia was rising to throw off her chains and when he, filled with the easy confidence of the young idealist, was playing a part in the process.

IV   *The Long Apprenticeship*

In the six years between the trip to Russia and his writing of *The Harbor*, the young man was engaged in a variety of activities and pursuits. Most important of these were his marriage and family life, his career as a short story and fiction writer, his work as a dramatist, and his involvement in socialism. Interestingly enough, each of these varied experiences made significant contributions toward his ultimate success with *The Harbor,* for the period was an apprenticeship in life, in writing, and in ideas.

Poole's marriage to Margaret Ann Winterbotham in February, 1907, brought him self-confidence, emotional security, and a substantial measure of happiness. His feelings of inadequacy, his persistent shyness in unfamiliar society, and particularly his belief that women did not find him attractive had always caused him considerable discomfort; one can, therefore, understand why winning the affection of an attractive Chicago heiress gave him the belief in himself which had long been lacking. But his luck was to be greater than he realized; Margaret Ann proved to be more than a status symbol or a temporary ego booster, for she had many of the same qualities he had admired in his mother. Her loyal support and encouragement of his work, the home she made for him and their children, the abiding security she represented—all these factors resulted in a remarkably happy existence for the young writer.

Soon after his return from Russia and throughout the early years of his marriage, Poole at last found himself a successful writer of short stories. George Lorimer, the editor of the *Saturday Evening Post,* liked his work so well that he printed five stories in a single year. Thus in a comparatively short time Poole found the success in fiction that had so long eluded him. For the most part, his writings of this period were "immigrant stories" that made extensive use of his knowledge of the dialect, customs, problems, and traits of the dozen or more nationalities he had studied on the East Side. In all, by the end of 1912 he had published over a dozen of these tales of life in the slums. In general, the "immigrant stories" are far superior to his other fiction published between 1905 and 1912; they are marked by understandable and well-developed characters, compelling themes that often approach genuine tragedy, and effective use of the local color of immigrant life. But even the very best of these tales seems dated today because in the last fifty years storytelling has become much more subtle and sophisticated. This change makes his style and technique, by comparison, appear amateurish.[12]

Doubtless encouraged by his new success as a fiction writer, he published in May, 1906, his first novel, *The Voice of the Street: A Story of Temptation.* One suspects that the work was a revision of a manuscript written during the settlement days because, like his first articles, it is based on his study of the lives of street boys. Dedicated to his mother, the novelette is essentially a dramatization of the conflict in the contemporary world between the materialists and the idealists who esteem culture, music, art, and beauty above financial gain. The plot traces the effect of these disparate values on the life and character of Lucky Jim, who begins his career as a singing newsboy and, after succumbing a number of times to the appeal of "easy money," eventually fulfills his destiny by becoming a concert artist.

The Voice of the Street is the worst book Poole ever wrote. The style is slovenly—full of slang and clichés, incorrect grammar, sentence fragments, awkward and incomprehensible phraseology, and crude and unrealistic dialogue. The characterization is unbelievable: both Gretchen, the pure and loyal maiden, and Fritz, the wise and kindly old musician—the friends of the hero—owe nothing to life and something to Dickens at his worst; and Lucky Jim's actions reveal him to be shallow, pompous, selfish, and weak-willed—not at all worthy of the hopes and sacrifices of his friends. As for the plot, it is as improbable in its general outlines as it is in specific details, and one cannot understand how anyone who knew about life in the slums and had observed people as they are could have produced such a fabrication of absurdities. Although the reviews were friendly except when they discussed the style,[13] Poole himself in a short time became critical of his first novel and in later years preferred to forget its existence. This failure was a valuable experience in that it taught the apprentice how much he did not yet know about writing—particularly about the demands of longer forms. At any rate, he waited seven years before making a second attempt; but in the interim he wrote constantly in order to improve his craftsmanship for the day when he would try again.

A part of his preparation was his career as a playwright in 1908 and 1909 and at intervals thereafter. His son, William, said that his father consciously undertook composing plays in order to attain skills in handling exposition, characterization, and, particularly, dialogue. Whatever his reasons, the effect of his writing perhaps a dozen full-length plays was to give invaluable practice in areas of composition in which he was, at best, untrained. It is therefore no accident that in his later novels he frequently used lengthy continuous scenes like those in plays and made dialogue his chief method of characterization.

Several extant manuscripts and some excellent reviews of performances provide a good look at Poole's strengths and weaknesses as a playwright. *None So Blind* (1910), for example, demonstrates skill in first-act exposition and in such mechanics as entrances and exits as well as in natural-sounding dialogue. The flaws, however, are overwhelming: the characters are either hackneyed stage types or subject to unbelievable changes in personality; the plot is full of melodrama and coincidence; and the theme is stated rather than dramatized. *A Man's Friends* (produced in 1913), owed its modest success to Poole's intimate knowledge of Tammany bosses and reform politicians, some of whom sat in on rehearsals and even suggested lines. He had clearly learned a great deal from his earlier failure, for the critics reported that the dialogue was clever and lively; the characterization, forceful and believable; the plot, logical and suspenseful. Even the didactic theme, the conflict between the demands of friendship and that of public morality, made its point without overt moralizing.

Take Your Medicine, an attack on scandal-mongering newspapers and legal injustices, composed in 1910 but not staged until 1916 in a revised form, is by far the best play. A comparison of the 1910 manuscript and the 1916 version gives convincing proof of how much he had learned in a few short years. The defects in character motivation, weak spots in the dialogue, and certain misguided attempts at satire are gone: instead, the portrayal of the two central characters is deepened and strengthened, and the heroine emerges as a real and understandable person—one of the first of Poole's many remarkable portraits of women. The small success of the play on the stage is not hard to understand: the picture of life presented was too real to appeal to a public that favored easy laughter, happy endings, and escape from the very thought-provoking issues that the author was discussing.

In addition to showing the remarkable pace of Poole's development as a writer, these plays also indicate that he was increas-

ingly using his artistic creations as a means of awakening his
public to the problems of the day. Although this practice may
have been a deliberate attempt to emulate such writers as Gorky
and Ibsen, the reason may well have been that he simply found
himself incapable of writing any material without including his
thoughts on social and political problems, especially in this period
when his sympathies with the oppressed were strongest. According to all accounts, Poole's vanished plays, like the ones which
survived, were attempts to dramatize ideas and present un-
palatable truths in the guise of entertainment. This search for
a new medium for encouraging reform was almost certain to fail
because audiences were not—and still are not—receptive to adult
education on the stage; as a result, Poole came to see the novel
as the only practical form in which to present his ideas—a form
which had the added advantage of reaching millions, not just
the regular patrons of a Boston, Philadelphia, or New York
theater.

As important as the development of his work during this period
was his gradual conversion to socialism, which, in turn, exer-
cised a profound influence on the ideas in *The Harbor*. In the
fall of 1908 Poole began to feel more and more drawn to the
conservative wing of the Socialist Party. He had long been in
substantial agreement with the socialists, and in many of his
published works he had advocated socialist reforms. In addition,
he had written articles in which he praised the work of "honor-
able men" who were devoting their lives to eliminating the
regnant social, political, and economic injustices; he lauded the
efforts of city planners, builders of art museums, and designers of
public playgrounds—men who were making positive and forceful
attempts to better their world and its people instead of exploiting
and brutalizing them.[14] Nevertheless, Poole still refused to join
the Socialist Party. It is possible that he felt that he could do
more good for the cause and receive a more sympathetic hearing
from the public if he were technically not affiliated with the
party, which many Americans viewed with suspicion and alarm.
Perhaps, too, he was afraid that he would be deprived of his
right to think for himself if he became a member. However, by
the fall of 1908, the party, under the leadership of Morris
Hillquit, had broadened and liberalized its creed and was purging itself of the old doctrinaires and practitioners of violence. Im-

pressed by the new "aura of respectability" and the similarity of his and Hillquit's moderate views, Poole joined a local in New York early in October.

At once he began to write for the party, over the next eight months contributing eighteen articles to the socialist newspaper, the *New York Call*. These pieces are fresh, vigorous, cheerfully partisan, and full of humorous scorn for the opposition's views; they doubtless delighted any readers who were sympathetic to the cause.[15] By writing such readable prose, Poole supported his belief that exposition of Marxist doctrine was not an effective way to reach the public; only a direct and lively appeal to their interest in people and to their natural sympathies could affect their votes and win support for reform. One can foresee, therefore, that when he wrote *The Harbor*, a socialist novel, he would not expound dogma; instead, he would bring that dogma to life in terms of human beings and human problems.

By the end of 1911 his apprenticeship was completed. Since September, 1905, he had been extremely productive: he had written a novel, a dozen plays, over fifty magazine pieces, and eighteen contributions to the *Call*. Very little of this material was of any consequence or literary value, but, in the process of writing it, he had gained the skill needed for his work to come.

CHAPTER 3

The Harbor

BY THE BEGINNING OF 1912 Poole was ready to make a
second attempt at a novel. He had already chosen the
general subject—his own analysis of the great changes taking
place in his country at that time. As he saw it, the most important
aspect of contemporary America was the growing danger of class
warfare. A combination of economic pressures and attempts to
crush the union movement was driving many workers into groups
like the "Wobblies," the Industrial Workers of the World, a
group with a reputation for dynamite bombs and brass knuckles.[1]
In January, 1912, what John Commons, the historian of the labor
movement, called "class war on a grand scale" came to the East
as the Wobblies turned to the "unorganized and grievously
treated workers in the textile industries." After a bitter three-
month strike at the American Woolen Company in Lawrence,
Massachusetts, the union, led by the famous William D. ("Big
Bill") Haywood, won its demands; and other New England
textile companies voluntarily raised wages rather than risk
similar defeats. But the event was more than a successful strike;
it was the first step toward class warfare. For the first time in
America an unorganized polyglot mass of unskilled workers had
united solidly behind a revolutionary leadership that preached
and practiced "direct action." As Commons said, "To the young
American *intelligentsia,* Lawrence was proof that a revolutionary
American labor movement, which had been forecast as inevitable
in the theoretical socialistic writings, was here at last. . . ."[2]

Poole, a socialist as well as an intellectual, could hardly have
been unaware of the significance of the struggle taking place
only a few hundred miles away; and it was apparently this sudden threat of imminent class warfare that stimulated him to start
work on the novel which he had been contemplating for many

years. He knew that immediate action was necessary to ameliorate the economic conditions which forced workers to rebel. But reform could come about only if the general public could be made to understand and sympathize with the lower classes and to demand helpful legislation. By using a sugar-coating of fiction he might perhaps be able to reach the voters with his message. Now all that he needed was a good plot with which to dramatize the situation.

I   *The Idea for a Novel*

The basic plan for *The Harbor* came to him in one short evening in the spring of 1912, shortly after the victory of the IWW at Lawrence. While a dinner guest in a stately old house that stood on a bluff in Brooklyn Heights overlooking New York's harbor, he discovered that the garden was built on the roof of an old warehouse. Poole found himself wishing that he had spent his childhood in such a house upon the threshold of the sea with this splendid view of the harbor; suddenly he realized that he had stumbled upon not only an ideal setting for his projected novel but also the chief character, the system of organization, and the unifying symbol of it:

> How would it be to try a story about just such a little boy in just such a place as this, with the harbor around him and even beneath, for his father would own that warehouse and pier and even the sailing ships that came. The boy would grow up and, as he grew—through good times, bad times, death, love, marriage, hope, despair, success and failure, pride, revolt—the harbor would keep changing, each time that he looked at it with his new eyes, changing like the boy himself, changing like this world I'd seen and through these forces I had seen; for wealth and poverty, labor, rebellion, and a whole world of trade and commerce, travel and adventure, were here! A harbor now wonderful, all romance, but again all grim and dull and flat; now friendly, now hostile.

He began work on his book by collecting background material. He filled his notebooks with detailed descriptions of Brooklyn Heights, of the harbor below, and of the ocean liners, the docks, and the people he saw there and had written about when he was a free-lance reporter.[3] Later on (perhaps in the early part of 1913) he was able to see the port as the longshoremen and the stokers saw it. This time his guide was one of Haywood's organizers, a twenty-five-year-old idealist who had left college to work as a stoker for two years and was now in the process of organizing a strike for the IWW. He took Poole down into the stokehole of an ocean liner and showed him the dreadful living and working conditions there. This experience gave Poole the material for the most vivid scene in *The Harbor,* and the young Wobbly, whom he called Joe Kramer in the novel, became the most believable of its three main characters.

The author had, of course, seen a large strike at close range during his stay at the Chicago stockyards in 1904, but he had never seen the process by which agitators initiated an uprising among unorganized laborers. Thus "Kramer" proved a godsend, for he was constantly meeting with groups of stokers, sailors, and longshoremen of all nations and races in anticipation of a strike in 1914. Soon Poole was recording the settings for his strike scenes and a rich body of detail about the men who would participate. He was particularly interested in recording the steps in the "awakening" of the common herd, the inspiring (and frightening) transition of a helpless and uncertain crowd of laborers into a united, fearless, and irresistible army. He had seen such a change take place during strikes, and there was no reason why it could not happen on a large scale and become a mass uprising of all the oppressed proletariat.

As he made his notes, two questions came to mind: did "such upheavals as these mean an end to the rule of the world by the keen minds of the men at the top?"; if the workers did overthrow the status quo and kill or exile the capitalists and their trained élite of planners and managers, could these men—so many of them broken and ignorant—really build the new world of their dreams? The leaders of the revolutionary labor movement were convinced that the workers could defeat their oppressors in a class war and that they could build a new social and economic order by themselves. Poole had ample reason to believe (as the capitalists did not) that they could destroy the old order, but he feared that the masses did not possess the skills needed to operate a modern civilization. The "people of the abyss" and their leaders had only a "blurred dream" and no real conception of the task before them, but Poole had seen with his own eyes the complexity of planning the world of the future.

For example, he went one day to the skyscraper office of the well-known civil engineer who was drawing the blueprints for the modernization of New York's harbor—the work that only men of intelligence and training could accomplish. Earlier, Poole had studied similar city planning done in Chicago—again by the men at the top. Unfortunately, these men, who were so important in the old order and who would be essential even in a classless society, would be the victims of a revolution because they did not believe in the power of the masses to destroy them, nor did they have any sense of the misery in which the lower classes lived. When the planners argued that their improvements eventually would eliminate the conditions that caused social unrest and strikes, Poole was convinced that they were sincere men and probably would, in time, substitute loading cranes for men's backs and oil burners for coal furnaces. He even took their point of view and presented it in the character of Dillon, the city planner in *The Harbor*. But he saw that their real interest was in achieving greater efficiency; living comfortable lives, they felt no need for immediate change; they could afford to be methodical, patient problem-solvers; this was an attitude those at the bottom of society would not forgive. Thus they would perish in a class war and with them would vanish the workers' chance of building a better world.

II *The Writing*

In 1912 the author went to New Hampshire for the summer and began to convert his notes and memories into a novel. He had no idea that he would spend two years at his task and that he would often become so discouraged that he would be ready to quit. His wife proved, however, to be "unfailing in encouragement and fruitful suggestions." The difficulty which Poole encountered in composing *The Harbor* apparently stemmed from the fact that he tried to write before he had arrived at a clear conception of his book. In later novels he began with an outline of the whole work and then laid out the story scene by scene before he began to compose.[4] But, according to his autobiography, in this case he had only a hazy notion of what he wanted to do; he also had trouble when he tried "to bring order and coherency" out of the notes he had accumulated. Clearly, he was often more hindered than helped by his abundant background material. He acquired new material for his book in February, 1913, when the Wobblies attempted to repeat their recent success in Massachusetts by organizing a strike in the Paterson, New Jersey, silk mills. He met Bill Haywood when he came to New York to take charge of the operation and was greatly impressed by the "magnetism" and courage of the great labor leader whom many called, with reason, the most dangerous man alive. Soon afterward he accompanied Haywood when he went to Paterson and addressed twenty thousand strikers in an open-air meeting.[5] This scene, which took place about March 8, became a part of the climax in *The Harbor,* and Haywood (like Michael Donnelly of the Butchers' Union) became a model for the fictional union leader, Jim Marsh. Thus the Paterson strike, which was ultimately crushed in August, provided the author with both firsthand material and the incentive to keep struggling with his recalcitrant novel.

The book finally fell into shape in the late fall of 1913 and was accepted by the Macmillan Company in the spring of 1914; however, the outbreak of the war in Europe at the end of July caused him to rewrite the ending to include the new crisis and the implications of the failure of the French and German socialists to prevent the conflict. Essentially, this addition predicts that, when the first glow of nationalistic enthusiasm fades, the revolutionary forces will come out of hiding, reorganize the now disillusioned workers, and end the conflict by overthrowing their masters. Apparently the original version had sent Kramer to organize new strikes in the United States; in the new ending he goes abroad instead. When the revision was completed, *The Harbor* was returned to the Macmillan Company and was published on February 3, 1915.

III *The Story*

The subject of Poole's most famous novel is the conversion of a young man to an active sympathy with the cause of the oppressed masses; it begins with his childhood and traces his growth against a background of historical events and social change. Book One deals with the first twenty-five years of the

life of Billy, the hero, and with the early influences on his attitudes. From his mother he learns to desire the "fine" things of
life—beauty, culture, art—and becomes determined to escape the
harbor, which represents the ugly, modern commercial world.
Later, in college, he is urged by his free-thinking classmate, Joe
Kramer, to learn about and write of the forces—economic,
political, and social—which bring violent changes to the contemporary world, of which New York harbor is a microcosm.
Billy, however, finds Kramer's views unsatisfyingly materialistic
and the subject unsuitable for an artist. During the next two
years Billy lives in Paris imitating in his writings the great
French authors of the past; Joe, as a newspaper reporter and
muckraker, studies labor unrest and the Russian Revolution,
events which he believes mark the beginning of a world-wide
social revolution.

Book Two describes Billy's struggle for success during the
period between 1905 and 1908 and shows his conversion to a
new religion—a belief in science or "Efficiency." When his mother
dies of cancer and his father is forced into bankruptcy, Billy returns to New York and starts earning a living by writing factual
stories about the harbor he so much detests. He soon becomes a
widely known, well-paid feature writer; marries Eleanore Dillon,
the daughter of a famous civil engineer and city planner; and
becomes one of the comfortable, complacent upper-middle class.
It is easy for him to accept the view of his father-in-law that
social and economic reform can be achieved only by "the men at
the top." Kramer tries to persuade Billy that there must be immediate reforms, that the masses can not and will not wait, that
a nation-wide labor war is near. Billy, nevertheless, continues to
take the "long-range view" since he believes that the masses are
capable only of destruction and must be restrained in the interests of progress.

Book Three covers the period between November, 1912, and
April, 1913, during which Billy becomes involved in a great
strike and changes sides. Kramer, now an embittered revolutionary, begins organizing stokers and longshoremen in preparation
for a general strike in the spring. He believes that eventually
such strikes will be able to paralyze the whole industrial world
and enable the workers to seize power. After Billy has witnessed

the shocking living and working conditions of the stokeholes and docks, his sympathies are aroused, and he agrees to write objective articles that will bring the matter to the attention of the public. Threatened with the loss of his job by his cautious, conservative editors, Billy stubbornly refuses to quit writing the truth.

When the strike actually begins, he finds to his amazement that a crude but democratic order is established and that violence is kept under control by the union leader, Jim Marsh. He wonders whether these people could perhaps run the world for themselves. He hopes that public opinion will force government intervention and a peaceful settlement. The owners, of course, have no such plans; using the police, a trumped-up murder charge, strike-breakers, and the militia, they overwhelm the workers. Billy, an innocent bystander, is one of those clubbed unconscious and jailed. In prison his conversion is complete: "and at last with a deep, warm certainty I felt myself where I belonged."

In Book Four, which tells of the events after the strike, Kramer, accused of murder, is freed by a jury and sets out for Europe to organize an underground movement against the capitalistic war that has begun there. Billy refuses to accept Kramer's narrow creed; but, with his wife's moral support, he dedicates himself to writing about social inequalities and injustices in order that average Americans like himself may learn their moral responsibility to bring about reform and the consequences of their failure to do so. He predicts that the strikers, now leaderless and scattered, will not forget their dream of owning the world in which they are now slaves; but, Billy warns, they can only destroy and cannot build the world they want. Because neither side can win a class war, a sensible solution must be found. Responsible leaders must teach the masses to use the ballot box instead of the bullet; at the same time, Americans of the middle and upper social classes must, like Billy, accept the facts that "life is growth and growth is change" and that one must be prepared to abandon old creeds and examine new ideas with an open and intelligent mind instead of blindly and automatically opposing any change in the status quo. Thus, reforms will be made, class war will be averted, and a more equitable social order will emerge.

IV *Characters and Plots*

The literary merit of *The Harbor* had little to do with its initial success. The shock and controversy aroused by Poole's interpretation of current events was by itself sufficient to attract readers during the next decade; but interest in his message naturally waned after New Deal legislation created a stable middle class that included much of the population and eliminated the threat of class war. Thereafter, the survival of *The Harbor* depended on Poole's success in his handling of characters, plot, style, dialogue, and background. He had—following the example of such socialistic novels as Upton Sinclair's *The Jungle* (1906), Charlotte Teller's *The Cage* (1907), and Arthur Bullard's *Comrade Yetta* (1913)—paid serious attention to such literary qualities.[6] Furthermore, he had tried to add depth to his book when he presented the central character as a part of a social group, involving him in a complex web of personal relationships with the supporting cast and in events other than those having to do with socialism. An examination of *The Harbor* will show how successful Poole's efforts were.

To begin, how good is the characterization? In general, one may say that almost all of the personages in the book are recognizable, consistent in their behavior, and adequately drawn. Only a few, however, become so alive that they remain with the reader after he closes the book; and, in several cases, the characters are rather weak. In particular, Billy, the central character, draws the most criticism. First of all, one tends to remember him as a disembodied voice or a shadowy observer, rather than as a real person. This impression, however, may be due to the fact that he is the first-person narrator; therefore, only on rare occasions does the reader see him "in the round" as he does the other people. However, at times (for example, when he is clubbed by a policeman), the use of this point of view is amply justified, for it enables the reader to associate with Billy and share his discovery of what it feels like to be a victim of social injustice.

A second subject of controversy about Billy's portrayal is whether the author adequately motivates his conversions first to "Efficiency" and then to reform. One may feel, after a first reading of *The Harbor*, that Billy changes his mind too readily; as a result, one may gain the impression that he is a weak-willed individual who follows anyone who is stronger, a muddled thinker unable to analyze the flaws in the arguments of others and swayed by appeals to the emotions, or merely a puppet who acts in a certain way because the plot requires him to do so. A second, more careful reading shows, however, that Billy's acceptance of Dillon's views is natural for a person of his social and economic status; that he consistently refuses to accept Kramer's extremist position; and that his final decision to pursue a middle course is based on logic and is achieved independently. It is, nevertheless, unfortunate that Poole did not make Billy's character less subject to misinterpretation because the average reader is not usually a careful one.

In evaluating the portrayal of the main character, one must take into consideration the view of the critics who assert that *The Harbor* is autobiographical and that Billy is really Ernest Poole.[7] In reality, he used only a few incidents from his own life and invented the rest, as a comparison of the events in the novel with those in Poole's autobiography, *The Bridge,* shows. The careers of the fictional Billy and Poole were actually quite different—as were their personalities and political opinions. This dissimilarity is particularly noticeable in their lives after college, when Billy became a politically conservative magazine writer while the author became an active member of the Socialist Party. In fact, Poole used some of his own experiences during this period, but he was telling of Joe Kramer's career, not Billy's. It is true that Billy is "converted," but he does not become a party member.

In other words, Billy's political views in 1913 are much like Poole's in 1904 before he became an active reformer. Billy is not Poole; he is an almost entirely fictional character, much like "the average American" to whom Poole, the socialist, was addressing *The Harbor*. There is one other interesting aspect of this question: years later when Poole was asked whether he was the hero of his novel, he quite correctly denied it; but he also asserted that Billy was much younger and much more radical than he had been at the time—a statement which is obviously an error—perhaps intentional; but, more likely, it was a slip of the memory.[8]

Eleanore is the least satisfactory of the main characters. For some obscure reason a reader never finds her as charming and

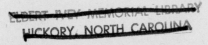

perfect as Billy does. She has, as one character points out, "no redeeming vices"[9] and is so cool and serene in time of trouble that one wonders whether there is any depth to her personality. The explanation for this faulty characterization may be that the author had not yet mastered his art; after all, the problem of portraying believable "good" women is one which has defeated many novelists, and Poole at the time was no exception. One may note in advance, however, that in a very few years he began to produce excellent characterizations of women; for instance, Jo in *With Eastern Eyes*, and Natalie in *Danger*.

Joe Kramer, unlike the other main characters, is clearly conceived, vividly executed, completely believable, and almost as complex as a real person. Indeed, he dominates the book whenever he appears and is the only one whose image remains permanently in the reader's mind. The portrait owes something of its reality to its real-life model, the young Wobbly organizer; but many of the best touches are the author's inventions. For example, he is careful to explain why Joe undergoes a complete change of character in the course of the novel: at first an idealistic adolescent seeking "Truth," he becomes increasingly bitter as his hopes for reform are defeated; his vision becomes clouded by his need for revenge, and finally he will not be satisfied until he destroys the old social order completely as a prelude to building a new one. Instead of "Truth," he can see only what he wants to believe, and he deliberately blinds himself to the weaknesses of the crowd. But Poole does not let the reader forget that there is still a warm-hearted human being beneath the surface of the hard-bitten revolutionary: Joe is still capable of falling in love, and he yearns like most people for some kind of personal happiness. *The Harbor* would be much less convincing if the author had contented himself with a picture of a labor organizer that excluded either his flaws or virtues and made no attempt to explain the forces that produced him.

Many of the supporting characters are well-drawn, even in their minor roles. Exceptions are Billy's mother, who is a rather conventional literary type, as is Sue, his sister. Jim Marsh, the union leader, has none of the vitality found in Joe; but in one scene, when silent and awed workers crowd around to see the famous agitator, one feels some of the personal magnetism that made men like Haywood natural leaders of workers. Billy's father appears in some excellent scenes, particularly when he uses every argument and trick at his command to save Sue from a marriage that will ruin her life. The reader is caught between admiration and revulsion when he describes in detail the process by which criminals like Joe are executed in the electric chair. But the most unforgettable minor character is Sally Marsh. Once a school-teacher and the daughter of one of the wealthiest men in her town, she is now middle-aged and embittered; she hates the "foreigners" who have taken her husband away from his family and his duty of supporting it. Wholly concerned with her own grievances, she has no sympathy for strikes, revolutions, or reform. All she wants is a home and a steady job for her husband. Sally Marsh, wife of a labor agitator and idealist, ironically is guided by the materialism and worldly aspirations of the upper and middle classes that her husband hopes to destroy. Undoubtedly she is one of the author's most inspired creations.

As noted, one of the features of *The Harbor* that distinguishes it from the usual socialistic novel is the author's attempt to broaden his story to include numerous "sub-plots" which may have no direct bearing on the central plot (the story of Billy's conversion) but which make his characters more understandable, give a picture of life in the era, and add engaging material to the book. Today, now that the main plot is hardly a burning issue, many of these sub-plots are of considerable interest. For instance, there is Billy's unfortunate encounter with a drunken prostitute who wears a garter on her fat leg. A few years later, as he and Eleanore are blissfully lying in a haystack he sees her garter, which has slipped from beneath her dress—and in an instant he feels such revulsion toward her that he runs away. Poole adds a final inspired touch to this episode: when the adult Billy meets the grown-up Eleanore and is conversing with her, the image of that garter and its foul connotations flashes across his mind. This revulsion against sex and "female filth," as Faulkner calls it, is a common experience among idealistic adolescent males; but Poole was one of the first writers to recognize its importance in shaping a character's attitudes. In fact, he included the passages about the garter against the advice of his friends, who felt that the subject was entirely too daring.

Another interesting sub-plot concerns Billy's father, who wasted his life fighting for a strong American Merchant Marine;

in his old age he talks of the glorious past of American shipping, thus giving the reader a chance to compare the days of the beautiful clipper ships with those of the dreary floating iron factories. Already mentioned is the importance of the plot involving Sue and Joe, by which the author shows Kramer as a complex and understandable person, and the equally good story of Mrs. Marsh, which provides a dramatic contrast between an idealist and his mate. Some of the sub-plots are essential to the main plot: for example, it is in part because of his love for Eleanore that Billy is converted to Dillon's "Efficiency" and becomes a political conservative; then, later on, he is encouraged to write his book when she proves to be a sympathetic, loyal helper who urges him to speak the truth even though it will unsettle their financial status. These added touches contribute to the novel by showing the hero as part of a social group as well as an actor in a dramatization of a social thesis.

V *The Style*

The style of *The Harbor* is uneven in quality, but a number of sections are extremely well written. Among the best are the pages devoted to the spirited arguments between Joe and Billy, the hero's first conversation with Eleanore, the visit to the stokehole, Mrs. Marsh's recounting of her experiences, the family quarrel between Sue and her father, and, of course, the events of the strike itself.

In these scenes the dialogue is well-handled, and certain lines could be spoken only by the character for whom they were tailored. The speeches of Billy's father, for example, have a distinctive rhythm. Elsewhere, when Marsh and Joe address the crowd, Poole captures the tempo of the talk of skilled handlers of men. The descriptions of the harbor, the ships, the events taking place in the strike headquarters, the sudden violence of street fighting—indeed, all of the background—show the hand of a competent reporter who had observed life and then reproduced it with photographic realism and richness of detail. Another aspect of the style of *The Harbor* is the use of profanity ("damn," "hell," and "God damn") to give realism to the dialogue—a rather daring inclusion for 1915. Also important is the use of slang and colloquial English, not only in the dialogue but in the narrative and descriptive passages as well—probably a result of the author's training as a journalist. But this use of informal English in a serious novel represented a break with tradition (although local color and humorous works had long been informal in style) and helped pave the way for many subsequent works in "American English."

Not all of *The Harbor* is well-written, however. The aspect of the book that most irritates and embarrasses the modern reader is the abundance of grammatical lapses, clichés, stilted speeches, and archaic slang (in the narrative sections as well as in the dialogue, where it is acceptable). More serious is the use in several places of the empty and pompous emotional language, usually found in exhortatory sermons or political harangue, that is surely out of place in a work of realistic fiction. The reader of these sections begins to wonder whether Poole is attempting to conceal a lack of specific ideas or is revealing absence of confidence in the power of his book to convince with facts alone. This device is particularly objectionable at the close of the book, when "a thick voice from the harbor" (the foghorn of a departing liner) says: "Make way, all you little men. Make way, all you habits and all you institutions, all you little creeds and gods. For I am the start of the voyage. . . . For I am your molder, I am strong—I am a surprise, I am a shock—I am a dazzling passion of hope—I am a grim executioner! I am reality—I am life! I am the book that has no end!"

One other important question merits consideration: are the political, social, and economic issues dramatized in *The Harbor* easily understood today? The answer is, unfortunately, that much of the meaning of the novel escapes the present generation. Even careful and well-informed readers often gain the impression that it is merely the story of a strike that failed, and they miss the point that it deals with class warfare and that Joe Kramer is an organizer for the IWW, a group dedicated to "direct action" and a communistic "government of the workers." The reason is that nowhere in *The Harbor* did Poole refer by name to Karl Marx, syndicalism, or the IWW, for to do so would have immediately inflamed his public's prejudices. Deprived of these clues, the modern reader, who probably does not even suspect that a revolutionary labor movement once existed in America, easily misses the point. When the book is taught to present-day college students (who also find the plight of the Joads in *The Grapes of Wrath* hard to grasp), it is necessary to give background information about the very matters which were obvious in 1915 and which made the book widely read and discussed.

VI *Evaluation*

After one has carefully examined all aspects of Poole's novel, only one conclusion is possible: *The Harbor* is something more than the best "radical novel" written during the period; it is more than a source book for the historian seeking an accurate picture of the views and events of that period; it is, by any standards, a good novel. The style is at times crude or dated, and the central issue is no longer important or fully comprehensible to most readers. But the important point is that his competent and sometimes brilliant characterization, sharply-etched backgrounds, well-done dialogue, and a wealth of human interest have made it a vital book of surprising durability. Although the author wrote even better novels in the future, *The Harbor,* with its solid craftsmanship, outlasted them all.

In its own time *The Harbor* made an almost unbelievable impact. The political conservatives rushed into print their denunciations of the "syndicalist" (communistic) views of the author, completely disregarding or overlooking the hero's middle-of-the-road position and his appeal for fair play and social evolution. Poole found himself attacked by such eminent voices as Paul Elmer More, the humanist, and Henry Mencken, the irate individualist, both of whom found their particular creeds in danger.[10] A cry of anguish was heard from college graduates when they read that their "education" was worthless; men of various backgrounds were angered by the fact that Kramer, Marsh, and Billy were apparently atheists who refused to accept traditional religions; the professional defenders of public morality protested against the scene involving the prostitute and the use of profanity, especially by children.

Equally loud were his defenders, who included a majority of the book reviewers and most of the reformers and liberals of the time—among them Theodore Roosevelt, William Allen White, Hamlin Garland, Lillian Wald, John Reed, Walter Lippmann, and the most respected novelist and critic of the period, William

Dean Howells. These readers called *The Harbor* a major contribution to American literature and praised its vitality, the vividness of its descriptive and narrative sections, and, of course, its
message. Letters poured in from liberals of other nations who
saw the novel as a foreshadowing of the coming of social justice
in the United States. Their interest is shown by the fact that
there were many English-language foreign editions as well as
translations into seven languages.[11]

The demand for the book in America was startling: it was the
eighth best-seller in 1915 and eventually sold over seventy-eight
thousand copies; there were twenty printings of the first edition,
two later hard-back editions, an expurgated high school version,
and four inexpensive paper-bound editions.[12] Coming as it did
during the era of Wilson's "New Freedom," the book found an
audience of young people who were greatly excited over the
ideas "blowing in the wind." It is hard to find a person of college
age at that time who has not read *The Harbor* and felt its effect
on his thinking. The book, because of its influence, came to be a
symbol of the Wilsonian Era; and recent novelists often mention
it in their fiction to show the political thought of the characters.
For example, in John Dos Passos' *U. S. A.*, one of the young
female radicals of the 1920's reads it; and in John P. Marquand's
H. M. Pulham, Esquire, the novel is observed in Marvin Myles'
bookcase in the same period. Marquand omitted Poole's name:
he obviously felt that the title of the book was sufficient to make
his point.[13] The great notoriety of *The Harbor* explains why, for
the next decade, the author could sell nearly everything he
wrote. There is even the possibility that the newly established
Pulitzer Prize bestowed on *His Family* two years later was in
part recognition of the importance of its predecessor.

Poole's reputation as a novelist was made almost overnight
by one novel. He was elected to membership in the National
Institute of Arts and Letters in 1916; his nomination by William
Allen White, Robert Bridges (editor of *Scribner's*), and A.
Lawrence Lowell (Harvard's president) "simply stated that he
was the author of *The Harbor*" and therefore eligible to be included in the membership of those citizens "qualified by notable
achievements in art, literature or music."[14] Soon after, he attained another mark of distinction when he was included in the
1916-1917 edition of *Who's Who in America*.

In recent years the reputation of *The Harbor* has declined along with that of its author. For the most part, the literary histories and critical books either make no reference to it or merely give it passing mention. Those which do discuss it are evenly divided on the question of whether *His Family* is its superior on purely literary grounds, but otherwise the consensus is that *The Harbor* is one of the best pieces of work to emerge from the muckraking era, "the best Socialist novel of all."[15]

This praise must be tempered, warns one critic, with the realization that not even the best was of the first rank, that "the Socialist novel of the century's first two decades belongs as completely to the past as the day of the Socialist Party itself," and that the genre has little to say to the present generation.[16]

There are, however, other critics who feel that *The Harbor*, because of its generous sympathies and intelligent criticism of life, is of permanent worth and should not be discarded.[17] If they are correct, then the novel may survive its present state of almost complete neglect by literary historians.

CHAPTER *4*

The Pulitzer Novel

SOON AFTER *The Harbor* was accepted for publication, Poole started work on a second major book—one that would earn him the first Pulitzer Prize ever awarded a novel and, at the same time, mark the high point of a literary career that had barely begun. In spite of the still fresh memories of the arduous labors and frustrations of the preceding two years—and even though he had no way of knowing how *The Harbor* would be received when it was published in February, 1915—he had decided to continue his new career as a novelist. Such a determined attitude was characteristic of Poole and, of course, accounts for his continued efforts in later years long after the eclipse of his literary reputation.

Work on *His Family* was interrupted by the outbreak of World War I at the end of July, and Poole was forced to re-examine his views both on socialism and on the meaning of the life and death of the individual human being. Inevitably, these thoughts influenced the content of the new novel. The first effect, however, had been the revision of the ending of *The Harbor*. Then, when he returned to the new book, he found himself increasingly distracted by the events abroad. No journalist, especially one who for a decade had reported on major upheavals, could long resist the desire to see firsthand and write about the greatest war in man's history. Likewise, no socialist could escape the need to understand the implications of what was happening: the socialist parties of Europe had failed to prevent a clash between capitalistic empires and, even worse, were actively supporting the forces of nationalism and aggression. The American Socialist Party was responding with a doggedly pacifistic stand; Poole, ever the questioner, wanted to see what war was like before he supported their view that peace at any price was preferable.[1]

I *The War Correspondent*

In November Poole sailed for Europe and spent three months observing the war from inside Germany as a correspondent for the *Saturday Evening Post*. His initial reaction to his tour was one of deep depression; everywhere there was death and destruction, but nowhere was there even nominal opposition to the war. The conflict actually appeared to stimulate the vitality, enthusiasm, and sense of dedication of those involved as nothing in peacetime had ever done. He saw little hope for the end of wars when men found excitement and joy in destruction. At last, however, he thought he saw a little hope; the strange energy and the eagerness to serve were not really products of war: instead, they were the normal condition of young people; and, because armies are concentrations of youths, these traits became extraordinarily common on the front lines. Perhaps these lessons of comradeship and devotion to high ideals would not be forgotten after the battles were over, and thus men would return to their old lives determined to build a better world. It was certain that the war would bring incalculable changes; it would so uproot the old ways of thinking, "the shams of peace," that the worn-out creeds would vanish, and men, their vision cleared, would experience a spiritual rebirth. Thus the sacrifices would not have been in vain.[2]

Considering Poole's long career as a reformer, one could expect no other attitude from him: a determined and unyielding optimist, he could always find grounds for hope; and, when he had found them, he would hold to them steadily thereafter. Nevertheless, in his reports from Europe and later in *His Family* there is little of youthful romanticism, and there is much of death and the thought of death. He had returned from the war a sadder and more thoughtful man; he was equipped to write of tragedy, of loss, and of the comforts man finds even in despair.

II *The Second Novel*

In June, 1915, inspired by the amazing success of *The Harbor*, Poole returned to his new manuscript. The book went well, with none of the problems which had plagued his earlier work, and was completed in New York by the end of the next summer. The speed and ease with which he worked indicate that by June, 1915, he apparently had in mind a clear conception of his goal— a novel about upper middle-class life in New York—and (if his later statements about his procedures are valid evidence) a neatly constructed outline of a plot.[3] This outline enabled him to divide the story into its main scenes and then to concentrate on the exposition, description, dialogue, and characterization in the individual sections. Such a methodical approach to novel writing, apparently adopted after his many months of confusion and false starts while composing *The Harbor*, had the additional advantage of allowing him to devote his time and energy to stylistic problems. The vast improvement in expression in *His Family* is undoubtedly a direct result of Poole's careful preparations.

The origin and the development of the plan for the novel are not entirely clear, but enough is known to suggest how his creative processes functioned. As early as 1908, when his wife was serving on the district school board, Poole became interested in education as a practical means of reshaping the world through its youth. He also saw the possibility of using schools and teachers in his writing, for he began to gather the material about them which went into *His Family* and into *Beggars' Gold*. It was probably at this time that he began to think of teachers and other school workers as, in a very real way, the spiritual parents of their numerous charges. From this notion developed the central theme of *His Family*: ". . . each man with a home of his own has two families, a little one inside his home and a boundless one outside. And to put this in novel form I built up a story about a father watching the lives of two grown daughters, one of them married and all wrapped up in her own small family; the other one mothering three thousand children as principal of a New York public school."

It should be remembered that a similar conflict of interests was also the theme of the play *A Man's Friends*, in which a crusading district attorney was the one who was faced with a choice between his private and public duties. In *His Family* the father, Roger Gale, is torn between these antagonistic loyalties; and, judging by the author's statements, he was originally invented to fill the role of a mediator between the central figures. However, as Poole continued to plan his novel,

Gale's part eventually developed into the most important one; and in the process, the old man became one of the writer's most authentic creations.

A number of other themes and characters found their way into the developing master plan, and nearly all of them grew out of the Great War. For example, Poole was keenly aware of the effect of the conflict on nearly every level of American life and on almost every type of individual. Many of the people in the New York tenements, he observed, found themselves jobless during the panic and economic recession which took place in the winter after the war started. Even the reasonably secure middle classes felt the pinch caused by events half a world away. Poole, who had tried to assess and analyze in *The Harbor* the meaning of current events, felt obliged to continue in his office as the chronicler of change—and, incidentally, to emphasize the idea that the nations of the modern world had grown so interdependent that none could avoid its responsibilities in global affairs. Poole also took note of the war's effect on a new class— profiteers who capitalized on the suffering of others and felt no moral restraints—and decided to incorporate these people in the novel. To do so, it appears, he increased the number of daughters from the original two to three; and he married the new one, Laura, to Harold Sloane, a handsome but unscrupulous capitalist.[4]

Death was a subject which seems to have obsessed Poole at this time. Because he no longer had any firm belief in life beyond the grave, the slaughter of countless youths seemed even more terrible than it would otherwise have been. Apparently he could not rest until he found some sort of substitute; and, as he had done with social dilemmas in *The Harbor*, he approached this personal problem by dramatizing it in *His Family*. It is no coincidence that Roger Gale ponders the question of immortality and, finally, in a vision at the moment of his demise, finds his answer—the continuation of the individual in the genes, memories, and character traits of his offspring. One may conclude that Poole's efforts to convince Roger of the sufficiency of this consolation were also an attempt to persuade himself.

His philosophical quandary may also have grown out of his relationship to John Geer, a crippled fifteen-year-old newsboy whom he met probably in 1913 or early 1914 and who died several years later. Geer made such a strong impression on Poole

that even twenty years afterward the author had not forgotten
the boy's fierce will to live, his courage, and his contagious
cheerfulness, despite the injury at the age of three months that
had caused constant pain ever since. John, who had refused to
enter an institution, earned his own living and planned for
the day when he would begin to study architecture.[5] The death
of this brave boy brought real and personal grief to Poole, and it
is no wonder that he tried to give him a kind of immortality by
working him into the plan of *His Family*.

III   *Technique, Mood, Style, Story*

Such were the origin and growth of the plot and the thematic
elements which went into the content of his second important
book. Also of interest is the origin of his choice of mood,
technique, and style. According to his own testimony, he planned
a book "about fresh new life" in order to give readers relief
from the horrors of the Great War. This is a surprising statement
to make about a story containing three deaths, loss and sorrow,
and family dissension; but perhaps he was referring to the fact
that the surviving children—the "new life"—carry on the dreams
and the traits of the dead. Possibly his conception of an inspirit-
ing subject owed much to the influence of William Dean
Howells, whose books he read and with whom he often talked.
Howells specialized in similar stories about the problems inherent
in the family and the marriage relationships of middle-class
Americans; and in his books the outlook (in spite of many
troubled pages) is predominantly "sunny" and optimistic. The
influence of another writer—Turgenev—is more obvious in Poole's
technique and style. Mrs. Poole recalled that her husband drew
his "quiet style" from the Russian, and perhaps the limited time
scheme of *His Family* also owes something to this master of the
"well-made" novel.

The second novel begins in April, 1913. Roger Gale, a widower
of sixty, awakens from the lethargy and despair in which he has
existed for sixteen years since the death of his wife and his subsequent loss of faith in personal immortality and in life itself.
He recalls his wife's deathbed request that he bring her news
of their children when he dies; and, realizing that he has only
a few years left, he forces himself to re-enter the world in order

to study his three grown daughters. Edith, thirty-five and maternal, keeps her husband, Bruce Cunningham, a handler of receiverships, busy supporting her family of four; she is completely engrossed in her children and would sacrifice everything for them.

Deborah, twenty-nine and the principal of a public school in the tenement area, is so devoted to her work with her three thousand students that she does not feel free to marry Allan Baird, a most patient fellow who has Roger's support in his courtship. The third daughter, the father's favorite, is Laura, gay, carefree, wasteful and basically heartless. Her goal in life is a "good time"; she has no intention of having children or of "settling down." Roger, who was reared in New Hampshire and has many "old fashioned" ideas, finds that it is too late to change Laura's attitudes and, a few months later, sees her marry Harold Sloane, a financier and heir to a fortune, obviously a man capable of supporting his bride in splendor.

Roger then turns his interest to Deborah in the hope of understanding her obsession with schools and, in some way, of persuading her to marry Allan. The results are good: the father learns of the vital role of schools in modern society and begins to feel a comradeship for the immigrant masses who have changed the face of the world in which he was born; Deborah, after a winter of cajolery and conniving by her whole family, agrees to marry. Nine days before the wedding is to take place, Edith's husband is struck and killed by an automobile. Edith is left without an income and with large debts; consequently, her father falls heir to her expensive household (now composed of five youngsters and several servants), which he moves into his old home near Washington Square. Deborah, of course, postpones her wedding indefinitely, dashing another of Roger's hopes.

The old man's troubles are, however, just beginning. His business, a newspaper clipping bureau, has suffered from his inattention over the years; and, when the war begins in Europe, he is almost forced to close it in the economic slump which follows. Only by mortgaging his beloved home and obtaining a loan at outrageous interest rates is he able to pay Edith's debts and provide the luxuries she feels are essential to her children's upbringing. It is only through the ingenuity of John Geer, a crippled boy whom Roger has taken into his office and his home, that the clipping bureau manages to survive the winter of 1914-15. Deborah, determined to alleviate the suffering among jobless slum dwellers, now cancels her matrimonial plans and wins Edith's enmity by devoting her income to her "family" instead of her nephews and nieces. The household is split even more when Edith expels John from the house on the grounds that he may infect her children with tuberculosis. Laura then adds her share to the family strife: after her husband grows rich on war profits, he begins to tire of her and turn to other women; when she, too, commits adultery, he divorces her. After a brief stay in Roger's house, she elopes to Italy with her lover, leaving Roger with a sense of defeat and Deborah disgusted with sex and marriage.

Early in the spring of 1915, when the old man learns that he has only a year to live, he begins to arrange his affairs and those of the two older daughters. He resolves to sell his house in order to settle Edith and her household on the old family farm in New Hampshire. Deborah is finally persuaded to marry; and, when the business improves under John's direction, the old house is saved and is given to the newlyweds as a wedding present. Before the next spring arrives, the Bairds have a child, thus giving Deborah her own little family and, at the same time, a deeper understanding of every woman and child in the great family of the world. John, uncomplaining to the end, precedes Roger in death and leaves his crutches to anyone who may need them. The old man, all of his affairs settled, succumbs to a stroke and sinks easily and gently into the dreams that come before death. In his final moments, as he feels himself drifting into a black and silent void, he thinks of the uncounted millions who have lived and died on the earth. Suddenly he sees all mankind as one great family struggling through the ages toward the light—and then before him stretches a vision of endless multitudes of children surging and spreading across the land toward a rising sun. At last he understands fully the true nature and extent of his family; overwhelmed by his reborn faith in life and by the certainty and sufficiency of a man's immortality in his offspring, he experiences "a clear sweet thrill of happiness" as he is drawn into the blinding light of the dawn.

His Family marks a definite advance over *The Harbor* in almost every way, and it is unquestionably one of the four or five of the writer's best books. Like its predecessor, it lacks the polish and "slickness" of his later works; but it has compelling vitality, strength, and sincerity. Furthermore, the novel embodies a deep and thoughtful probing of the problems of human relationships and an awareness of the beauty and tragic shortness of life which are missing in the large-scale treatment of sweeping social and economic forces and of masses of men in *The Harbor*. Admittedly, *His Family*, because of its subject, does not offer the excitement and emotional stimulation of a novel about class warfare; but unless the reader has an aversion to "genteel realism" like that of Howells and Tarkington, he has to admit that Poole had surpassed his previous achievement.

The author's style had definitely improved and shows signs of the persistent revision on which Poole relied. The descriptive passages are usually free of clichés and hazy images, even when the author is feeling poetic or trying to establish a mood. Most of the slang and disreputable grammar of his previous writing has been replaced by more formal prose except for the inevitable dangling modifiers. The most convincing writing, however, is found in the dialogue, which is occasionally so close to the conversations of everyday life that it simulates the banality of a literal transcription. Frequently the speeches are so individualized and characteristic of the speaker that Poole does not bother to identify him. Exceptionally good are the scenes in which the sisters quarrel, tossing chilly sarcasm and venomous comments at one another; almost as effective are the fumbling attempts of their father to make his views accepted or understood—only to realize at last that he is failing to communicate with his own children. Of course, not all of the novel is a stylistic triumph. Many pages are flat and dull, too slow-moving to hold the attention. The most annoying flaw is the author's word-for-word repetition of his theme at regular intervals so that the less alert minds in his audience will not miss the philosophical thesis. And, finally, there is the rhetorical close so typical of Poole's early books—a burst of splendid emotion and high-sounding phrases calculated to leave the reader in an elevated frame of mind.

When judged on matters of technique, *His Family*, with its limited time scheme, few characters, and restricted point of view, is an advance over *The Harbor*. Poole limits the story of

Roger Gale to the last thirty-seven months of his life, telescopes earlier happenings into brief recollections, and advances his plot with scenes and dialogue rather than with authorial narrative. This method gives the book the leisurely pace necessary for adequate characterization and the picturing of middle-class lives and everyday problems. For the most part, Poole restricts himself to presenting only those scenes in which Roger appears, and he concentrates on the old man's actions and thoughts; the method of narration is like that of Henry James in *The Ambassadors*, in which the author tells nothing that his character, Strether, does not learn. Unfortunately for the readers who prefer consistency in such matters, Poole occasionally reverts to the device of the omniscient author to bring in scenes outside of Roger's knowledge—certainly an unsportsmanlike action, and one repeated in many subsequent novels.

The characterization is the strongest element of the book; and the first sixty-nine pages, in which the cast is introduced and delineated, could stand alone as proof of Poole's ability. Roger Gale is a creation worthy of Howells—a complex, many-sided personality as real as life itself. Unlike some of Poole's heroes, who are either the author in disguise or the spokesman for his ideas, Gale is independent of his maker. Although he is exposed to new ideas, he prefers his old-fashioned concepts and is motivated in his actions solely by the ideals he learned as a child in New Hampshire. The reader soon becomes intimately acquainted with the old man through his actions and his innermost thoughts, but because Poole also shows—usually through dialogue—what other people think of Gale, the reader's sympathies are tempered by the realization that, in the eyes of his acquaintances, Roger is a relic of the past: a slightly senile old fellow whose peculiarities are to be smiled at and whose opinions are to be heard but not heeded. The reader thus is left to make up his own mind about Gale, but inevitably he comes to admire and respect him—even to be deeply moved by his death.

Perhaps an even more remarkable accomplishment is the novelist's portrayal of the women in his story. Both Deborah and Edith are sharply individualized in physical appearance, patterns of thinking, and speech mannerisms; yet both are clearly representative of their sex. Their lives are ego-centered; their decisions are usually emotional judgments; they are at times almost unbelievably petty and perverse. Edith with her single-minded devotion to her children is probably more convincing than the idealistic Deborah, perhaps because the Ediths of the world far outnumber the Deborahs and are therefore more easily evoked in a reader's mind. Laura, the luxury-loving third daughter and the prototype for Poole's later amoral female pseudo-intellectuals, is presented vividly; but the characterization lacks the depth of that of her sisters—perhaps because her "chicken brain" has no depth, perhaps because the author disliked her type intensely.

The treatment of the secondary personages—Bruce Cunningham, Allan Baird, and John Geer—is more than adequate even though they appear less often than the others. Bruce, in particular, is so real that the book seems decidedly empty after he is killed. Allan, unfortunately, has a trait all too common in Poole's men—the masochistic tendency to suffer long in the courtship of the women of their choice; otherwise, he appears to be a normal, intelligent human being. As for John, his presentation is somewhat weakened by the author's emphasis on his heroism and cheerfulness; but, on the whole, he, like the other minor figures, is a convincing portrayal.

When one recalls Poole's partiality to including ideas in his fiction and remembers that *His Family* was at its inception a book about education, one would expect to find the novel burdened with social messages, the plot hindered by tedious sections of doctrine placed in the mouths of helpless characters. Luckily, such is not the case. The family, its problems, quarrels, and joys are the central matter in the book and occupy most of the pages. The role of education in the world and the conflict between private and public responsibilities are worked into the novel inconspicuously and dramatized so naturally that no one is annoyed by their presence. As a matter of fact, it is the personal theme—the search for immortality—which is awkwardly handled and repetitious.

Thematically, *His Family* is the first—but not the last—of Poole's novels to present his belief that life in the city is unnatural, rootless, and vitiating and that only by a physical return to the country and a spiritual return to its simple values and ideals can a full, happy existence be attained. Lest anyone suggest that the idea is trite, it must be said in defense of the author that this is not a literary affectation or the vicarious longing of a city dweller for a quiet he could never have endured; Poole, beginning in 1912, usually took refuge during the summer in his cottage in the New Hampshire mountains. Thus, this idea, like many of his, while not original or striking, was nevertheless a genuine conviction.

A final point is the novelist's treatment of sex in this novel. As in *The Harbor*, he included material which must have shocked the puritan element. For example, the subject of Laura's adultery is discussed openly and frankly by the characters, but it is not described in detail by the author as it would be in a present-day novel. Roger's pre-marital adventures with prostitutes and the unsatisfying coldness of his wife are mentioned only briefly, but they are certainly suggestive and far more daring than anything in the novels of Howells. It is clear, however, that Poole used this material, not to shock his readers, but to give them a fuller understanding of a character and to present a serious comment on human relationships. In later years, as censorship lessened and public taste became more liberal, he became much more explicit about sex; but he remained true to his artistic creed and made no attempt to imitate the clinical descriptions favored by the naturalists. Furthermore, although he apparently was acquainted quite early with Freud, Poole never altered his view of human existence to place sex at the center; he was content to view this drive as an important part, but not as the whole of the life of a human being.

IV   *Reception*

His Family was published first in serial form in *Everybody's* from September, 1916, to May, 1917; when it appeared in book form, it immediately met with great success. Many of the reviewers called it the outstanding book of the year and gave particular praise to the character portrayal, which, they said, equaled or surpassed that of William Dean Howells. There were, however, some who criticized the stylistic flaws and were disappointed that the book was not "another *Harbor*"; that is, it was lacking in epic scope and significance. The public response was so great that *His Family* eventually sold over thirty-three thousand copies, became the eighth best-seller of the year, and later was issued in two paper-backed editions.[6] These statistics and the fact that the book was made available to a large audience in its magazine form indicate that it was probably the author's most widely read novel.

His Family received several impressive awards. It was voted the most important novel of 1917 by a jury selecting titles for the National Arts Club Exhibit.[7] Then, on June 4, 1918, Poole's book received the first Pulitzer Prize ever awarded a novel: "For the American novel published during the year which shall best present the wholesome atmosphere of American life and the highest standard of American manners and manhood, $1,000."[8]

This prize for *His Family* and the reputation of *The Harbor* are Poole's claims to recognition today. All the novels he wrote afterwards were compared with them; and, according to the critics, none ever equaled these early efforts.

V His Second Wife

Poole began work upon his next novel in the fall of 1916. Little is known about the writing of the story except that it was probably finished by the end of March, 1917, when he began to devote all of his time to activities connected with the war effort, and that the work was interrupted in November and December by the production of *Take Your Medicine* in Boston. Thus only seven months were devoted to the development of the idea, writing, and revision. There is reason to believe that he was responding either to his own desire to capitalize on the success of the earlier books or to pressure from his publishers and hence had to work faster than he should have. Thus he wasted a rather provocative idea for a book—the problems faced by the woman who marries the widower of a very attractive predecessor.

The novel first appeared as a serial, *Two Wives*, in *McClure's Magazine* from October, 1917, to May, 1918. It received publication in book form on May 14, 1918, as *His Second Wife*. The title figure, Ethel Knight, is an attractive twenty-two-year-old who comes from a small town in Ohio to live with her married sister in New York City after their father's death. She hopes that life in the big city will bring her cultural advantages and cultivated friends, an opportunity to develop into the well-informed, independent sophisticate known as the "New Woman."

Her sister Amy, however, has other plans for her: she begins at once to train Ethel in the art of hunting a rich husband. Wealth and social prominence, Amy believes, are the most important aspects of life in New York; and the best way for a woman to achieve these goals is to marry a wealthy man and use feminine wiles to encourage him to acquire even more money. Amy, it is obvious, has a firm hold on her husband, Joe Lanier, a building contractor and real estate speculator, whom she has persuaded to give up creative work in architecture for more remunerative activities.

Barely a month after her sister's arrival, Amy dies suddenly and horribly of ptomaine poisoning. Ethel stays on in the Lanier's apartment to care for her sister's baby; and, in the ensuing year, she gradually and unintentionally supplants Amy in Joe's affections. After their marriage she discovers that she must compete not only with the memory of Amy's sensual body but also with the materialistic ideals which Amy had instilled in her husband. Resolving to resurrect his interest in creative work, Ethel, without Joe's knowledge, concocts a series of schemes to win back his former friends, a coterie of intellectuals whom Amy had forced him to drop. All goes well until Joe gets the mistaken impression that she is having a love affair behind his back; in the end, the truth is revealed to the jealous husband. Joe, after a nervous breakdown induced by his worry over his wife's behavior, is saved from materialism; and the reunited couple sets out for a Paris holiday. Ahead of them lies the rich, full life which Ethel had planned when she came to the city three years earlier.

His Second Wife is one of Poole's least satisfying productions and a surprising successor to *The Harbor* and *His Family*. The novel is carelessly and sloppily written, filled with embarrassingly flat dialogue, and often marred by trite and uninspired diction. It is one of the novelist's few attempts to devise a book in which the plot is a major concern. His decision to develop a complex narrative may have resulted from his recent writing for the stage, a medium in which multifarious complications are fairly common. In *His Second Wife* he succeeded only in annoying the reader, and the novel loses its directness because there is too much tying and untying of knots. Furthermore, the death of Amy, one of the few powerful scenes, is obviously a mere device to get the story under way. Worst of all, except for Ethel, the characters are nothing but names or, at best, only shadowy figures.

One of the few successful aspects of *His Second Wife* is the technique used to present Ethel. The narrative is focused on the heroine and concerns itself with her actions and especially with her inner soliloquies, self-dramatizations, and mood changes. In a very short time he limns an indelible impression of her (His method is similar to that used in *His Family*, and in Stephen Crane's *The Red Badge of Courage* as well). But even here he mars his achievement by his carelessness, for the reader is certain to be exasperated by the unnecessary, abrupt, and momentary transitions into the thoughts of other characters, a defect also found in *His Family*.

Ethel, admittedly, is unforgettably delineated. Unfortunately, she does not fit the qualifications of the heroine of a crusade against materialism. She is, because of her small-town upbringing, lacking in poise when faced with unfamiliar situations and new acquaintances; and she has only a vague and confused conception of what she is seeking. These flaws might be forgiven except for the fact that she is inordinately self-centered and thoughtless of the feelings of others, shallow and silly even in her deepest thoughts, and given to elaborate rationalizations. For example, when Joe is tormented by the suspicion of her infidelity, which her actions have aroused, she delays giving him an explanation for three days on the self-righteous grounds that he should trust her implicitly.

Ethel also aspires to become the "Modern Woman," but she is intellectually incapable of such an achievement; and her interest in suffrage fades when she is assigned clerical work and discovers that the task is not as glamorous as she had hoped. Her disinclination to work also cuts short her abortive attempt to earn her own living as a typist, and after her marriage she acquires tastes and desires that are almost as expensive as those of her sister. Perhaps her most irritating trait is her attitude toward sex: a prude, she imagines that every man in sight is lusting after her body. Yet, like Richardson's Pamela, she does not hesitate to use her physical attractiveness to her own advantage; she wears clothing designed to excite in men the very emotions she so earnestly deplores. It is difficult to imagine such a creature as a force capable of producing intellectual and esthetic enlightenment or a more spiritual way of life. But Poole nowhere indicates that he is conscious of the incongruity of her roles. In later novels—*Silent Storms, Great Winds, The Destroyer, Millions, The Avalanche*—this type of woman is under attack by the author. But in *His Second Wife* a reader always has the nagging fear that Poole admires his heroine as a brainy, clever, well-adjusted example of young American womanhood.

There are four main themes in this novel, all competing for attention with varying success. The first is the problem facing a man's second wife when she must cope with an idealized memory of her predecessor. In the early pages this awkward situation is handled rather convincingly, but the idea is dropped for long periods and loses its dramatic effectiveness. Too often the novelist tells of Amy's influence but does not bother to show it in action, and the reader's interest soon fades. The second theme concerns the need for people to find "their calling" in a materialistic world. The presentation of this theme is unsatisfactory because the schemes of the wife are ridiculous, and she herself can hardly be called a good influence.

A third major element is the role of sex in a modern urban society. When one considers the religiosity and prudery of the period, the treatment of such matters was both courageous and frank. Today this story seems fairly innocent, but it doubtless owed a part of its large sales to its "scandalous" material. The fourth theme is the hollowness of existence in contemporary New York. Life there is without roots, religion, or genuine friendship, says Poole, who did not approve of the tinsel of social life or of marriages without the basic ties of companionship and mutual respect. He makes his point so well that one begins to lose interest in these insincere people and their pointless maneuverings. Only occasionally does one find incidents which have the air of genuine emotion and reality about them. In one digression, for example, a little boy in a park asks his father to buy him some peanuts. "Like hell I will," responds the father, revealing a great deal about himself and the life that a harassed parent leads.

The response of the critics to *His Second Wife* was disappointment and regret that Poole had failed to equal his two previous novels. They found only commonplace and conventional stock characters, not the real human beings they had expected; and the plot seemed trivial and obvious, little more than a padded short story. Even worse for his reputation, some voiced their suspicions that the book was either an early experiment or a hasty attempt to meet the demand created by the previous successes. Whether the charge was true or not, the label of "hack writer" proved hard to lose. Although *His Second Wife* sold nearly twenty thousand copies, a record topped only by *The Harbor* and *His Family,* even the friendly critics held to their view that it had appeal only for the semi-literate, scandal-mongering magazine public. His enemies, of course, were unable to conceal their glee: as Mencken said, "It was a cheap, a hollow, and, in places, almost an idiotic book." Poole never forgave him.[9] The fact remains, however, that he should never have allowed the publication of a book which sullied the reputation of two outstanding books and the many yet to be published.

CHAPTER 5

The War and After

IN APRIL, 1917, the World War came to America; Poole, who
had stubbornly refused to believe that he and his country
would become involved, now found himself taking part in or observing some of the most significant events of the time. In the
next two and a half years he participated in the virtual wrecking
of the Socialist Party; he served the Wilson administration's war
effort as an apologist and propagandist; and he visited Russia
as a correspondent and unofficial government agent during the
short life of the Kerensky Republic. Much of his energy during
this period went into unsigned press releases or time-consuming
administrative work, but he did produce a small body of assorted
articles and three books. *"The Dark People": Russia's Crisis*
(1918) and *The Village: Russian Impressions* (1918) were based
on his magazine reports; and *Blind* (1920) dramatized the
authors' own experiences and his troubled thoughts about the
unforeseen problems caused by the Great War. These writings
are significant records of the times and Poole's reactions even
though they did little to enhance his literary reputation.

I *The Choice*

When Congress declared war on Germany and her allies,
Poole was forced to make a painful decision. As a socialist, could
he support a war, especially after he had seen its horror at first
hand? The Socialist Party began to split into two violently dis-
senting groups as its members debated the issue. Poole began to
suspect that many who purported to be pacifists were really
German sympathizers or else did not understand the situation in

Europe. He became convinced that America had been forced to intervene in order to save civilization; and, after Hillquit called upon the workers to refuse to fight in the capitalists' war, Poole, Arthur Bullard, W. E. Walling, C. E. Russell, Robert Hunter, J. G. Phelps Stokes, and others split from the party.

Perhaps they had chosen the wiser course, for the government soon afterward raided the various headquarters of the party, suppressed socialist periodicals, stamped out the IWW, and put Eugene Debs in prison.[1] On May 8, 1917, Poole, Walling, Russell, and other prominent socialists met in Washington, D.C., and denounced the forthcoming Stockholm International Socialist Conference as a plot of the Kaiser to trick the Russian delegates into working for a separate peace. The German delegates, they insisted in their statement to the newspapers, were not really socialists: all the real German socialists were in jail.[2] It did not occur to Poole that, in a sense, the same situation existed in the United States.

Determined to give active support to the war effort, he accepted with enthusiasm a post on George Creel's Committee on Public Information. With the exception of the summer months of 1917, he worked steadily thereafter in the process known to its advocates as "mobilizing the mind and spirit of America" and to its opponents as "thought control." In retrospect, it is truly ironical that Poole, who had been shocked in 1914 by the German government's control of the minds of its people, should have allied himself with Americans dedicated to convincing citizens that the war was a good thing and that anyone who opposed the war or refused to fight was a foe who deserved prison or worse. In his defense, however, it must be said that he had no idea that his work would contribute to the destruction for many years of tolerance and free speech in this country.

II Defense of War

Poole's first task for Creel was the popularization of an introduction Bullard had just written for a proposed State Department "White Book"—a defense of America's decision to declare war and an exposition of the actions of Germany which had left the government no alternative. He took Bullard's typescript and spent five weeks in an attempt "to make it all so plain and clear that every enlisted man or boy can read it and know what he's fighting for." *How the War Came to America* was translated into twelve languages, and over six million copies were printed and distributed. According to Creel, "In authoritative judgment it stands today as the most moderate, reasoned, and permanent pamphlet put out by any government engaged in the war. And the way it was prepared was a cheering demonstration of citizens of a democracy doing its own defending and defining of its ideals." To Creel, the success was in a large part a tribute to "Poole, with his clear, democratic vision."[3]

Poole's other writings for the war effort included magazine publicity for Herbert Hoover's Food Administration, widely circulated articles on patriotism in the army and navy, and two statements of his personal convictions about the war. In "Why I Am No Longer a Pacifist," he told in detail of his growing conviction that, whatever the causes had been, the war had developed into a struggle to the death between the liberal people of the world and the forces dedicated to the crushing of liberty. He also declared that he had never been a real pacifist except in wars of aggression started by capitalists; the use of force, he felt, was morally defensible in a struggle against oppression. The second article, "The Fighters and the Haters," in which he spoke for a group called "The Vigilantes," was an attempt to expose self-styled patriots: only those who wanted peace without revenge were the true fighters; the haters would make Americans lose sight of their goals.[4] Unhappily, the warning went unheeded by the general public; it soon supported the seekers of vengeance at Versailles.

III *Foreign Press Service*

His most valuable service to the government began in November, 1917, when George Creel asked him to take part in the Foreign Press Service. The purpose of this organization was to unleash a flood of American propaganda in the newspapers of every foreign nation. There were three divisions—cable news, moving pictures, and mail-feature service; Poole organized the third branch. By the spring of 1918 he had over two hundred people at work writing news stories about America. Most of them were brief rewrites of news and magazine articles, but they covered nearly every aspect of American life and amounted to seventy or eighty thousand words weekly. By the end of the war the Americans, without buying space in foreign newspapers, had placed more propaganda in them than any other government. Undoubtedly, much of the credit belongs to Poole, who knew the kind of material editors wanted: he always emphasized the human interest; he knew how to underplay America's role in order to avoid resentment abroad; and, in spite of the interference of "super-patriots," he published the truth and refused to "whitewash" the failings in American life.[5]

In July, 1917, five months before organizing the mail-feature division of the Foreign Press Service, Poole made his second trip to Russia. The regime of the Czar had been overthrown in March, and he wanted to see the country now that the dream of 1905 had been fulfilled. He also wanted to collect material for a series of articles about "Russia's long struggle to be free" in order to win the support of the American public for Kerensky's new republic and for Wilson's plan to keep Russia in the war with large amounts of "foreign aid." When he arrived in Petrograd, he found only chaos; and he saw immediately that Kerensky, dedicated to keeping Russia in the war and to achieving gradual reforms through democratic processes, was being deliberately undermined by the communists with their promises of a quick end of the hated war and immediate distribution of land to the peasants. They seemed almost certain to seize power; but Poole saw hope that American donations of food and other aid would keep the Kerensky government in power and thereby foil the communist plan to sign a separate peace with Germany. Thus it was essential that the American public be persuaded to invest heavily in Russia; and, to do his part, Poole resolved to pursue the point in both articles and books. Furthermore, since Russia was needed so desperately in the war, he decided to urge a policy of friendship even if "the Reds" took over the government because it would encourage them to change their attitude toward the Allies.

Although the discouraging aspects of the situation were the most evident ones, he also reported on indications that constructive forces were at work. At the insistence of old friends like Katharine Breshkovsky, he accompanied his interpreter, Tarasov, on a tour of the villages, where, it was affirmed, the important revolution—a social and economic rather than a political one—was taking form. In fact, it was said, the triumph of the communist doctrines in the cities would barely affect the lives of the peasants, who made up the vast majority of the population; thus, a meaningful revolution in Russia could come only through education of the people and a vast improvement in agricultural methods. He was surprised to find great enthusiasm among the villagers for practical projects that would bring about such a change. The peasants were attempting to obtain modern farm equipment and were setting up a union of cooperatives; but probably the most encouraging development in the villages was the effort by a few determined schoolteachers to show the peasants how to read, write, and solve simple problems of arithmetic. Impressed by their accomplishments, Poole, already converted to the idea that education could save the world, resolved on his return home to urge American help for Russian schoolteachers.

During his tour of the provinces, a trip which ranged from villages on the Volga to those bordering Finland, Poole met two men who were to have a permanent effect on his thinking. One was Kraychok, a village sorcerer. Tarasov told the reporter of the strange hypnotic power which the old man used to cure the sick and to assist in childbirth. The visit to the hut of Kraychok made a deep impression on Poole and accounts in part for his later interest, particularly in the novel *The Avalanche*, in the powers (telepathy, clairvoyance, hypnotic control) which, we are told, lie unexploited in men's minds. The other man who influenced him was an elderly Volga fisherman who told him a parable. According to an old folk story, he said, God once walked across the wilderness of the sky exhaling white puffs of vapor in the cold, making little clouds which faded in a moment. One of those clouds is the Milky Way; and what to mankind is millions of years is only a moment in God's time. Therefore, said the fisherman, the little men who worry over their insignificant plans and problems should look up at the sky, remember this story, and be silent and at peace in their minds. Poole never forgot this parable and used it not only in two of his novels—*With Eastern Eyes* and *Great Winds*—but also as a kind of sedative to his own spirit in the troubled decades that were to come.

IV Books about Russia

Eight articles describing his experiences and giving his opinions about Russia's future appeared in several magazines in the next year; six of these were gathered into a book called *"The Dark People": Russia's Crisis*. The work is valuable as a firsthand report on conditions prevalent in the summer of 1917 in the Russian government, army, industrial and railroad systems, church, and peasant communities. But Poole had no way of knowing which trends would be significant, and many of his evaluations soon proved to be incorrect. The book should, therefore, be read along with a good history of the fall of the Kerensky government and with John Reed's *Ten Days That Shook the World*. Another weakness is that his account of the various conflicting creeds makes unexciting reading. He had deliberately avoided the dogmatic leaders of the various factions and interviewed, instead, representative members of each in order to avoid abstract theories and to show how ordinary people reacted to events. His material, nevertheless, lacks human interest; it is repetitious and poorly organized, sometimes dreary. A story of an indomitable and spirited peasant girl in the last chapter is one of the few portions with intrinsic literary value and genuine human appeal. Without a doubt, the articles which Poole wrote in 1905 are much better than these, which were penned hurriedly in the desperate hope that democracy would survive, and which are characterized by naïve optimism rather than objective evaluation.

His expectation that the book might sway American foreign policy brought him only disappointment. Although the reviewers praised the quality of the reporting and seemingly accepted his views, and the public bought out several reprintings by March, 1920[6] (*"The Dark People"* eventually sold over six thousand copies), the American aid was too little and too late; and it ended when the Bolsheviks took power.

A second work based on Poole's trip to Russia, *The Village: Russian Impressions*, was published on November 6, 1918; excerpts from it appeared in several magazines. The book covers the last two weeks of the stay in Russia and begins with the escape of Poole and Tarasov from the turmoil of the city to the countryside. Colorful descriptions of crowded trains and primi-

tive villages are interspersed with speculations on Russia's future
and stories of life in the days before 1900. Gradually the writer
paints a picture of the typical Russian as he saw him: lovable
and fascinating, full of humor, often impractical, a great talker.
Also included are stories of the priests and teachers who devoted their lives to raising the peasant to manhood through
practical education and cooperative enterprises, as well as an
account of the village sorcerer who had learned to use the
mysterious extra-sensory powers of the mind.

Clearly a better effort than *"The Dark People,"* this well-
written little book is charming in its pictures of Russian life and
character and often engrossing in its accounts of what self-
sacrificing men can do. Its dialogue is excellent, its humor re-
freshing and bright. Poole was always at his best when he had
to do with human beings instead of political doctrines and abstract ideologies, and he seemingly improved stylistically when
he enjoyed his subject matter.

The reviewers in 1918 and 1919 found themselves swamped
by a large number of works on Russia, a fact which may account
for the little attention they gave *The Village*. One critic, however, lauded the sense of reality, the artistry of the style, and
the understanding of Russia shown by the author; he called the
result a "memorable book." Public response was equally
enthusiastic: several printings became necessary,[7] and eventually
over nine thousand copies were sold. Otto Mallery has said that
the book was used as a model of style in several high schools
and colleges, and the author himself considered it one of his best
pieces of writing.[8] Even today one finds *The Village* exceptionally readable.

V *Aftermath of World War I*

The end of the war found Poole exhausted and disheartened.
His work with the Foreign Press Service had consumed so much
of his energy that he almost had a nervous breakdown before it
ended. Adding to his worries, his wife and their children became
seriously ill during the influenza epidemic in the last weeks of
the war. Approaching forty, he no longer had his former re-
silience of body or spirit. It is little wonder that he was ill-
prepared for the aftermath of the war or that, after years of un-

flagging idealism and optimism, he was overcome by despair and believed that all of his efforts had ended in humiliating defeat.

Even the most cheerful liberals found the events after the Armistice appalling, and it is a historical fact that in those bleak days many socialists and reformers—disillusioned, disgusted, perhaps even frightened—withdrew from the liberal movement. To win the war it had seemed essential to eliminate all critics of the government—and, in the process, leading socialists and pacifists were sentenced to long terms in Federal prisons. Many people regretted these excesses but assured themselves that, after the world was made safe for democracy, all injustices would be remedied. Instead, after the war the country was swept by the great "Red Scare," lynchings of Wobblies, mob action by "patriotic" servicemen against peaceful meetings of socialists, and persecution of minorities. A dozen years would pass before liberals would again be accepted and understood by the majority of their fellow Americans.[9]

Abroad, the situation was equally disheartening. The United States began to press for payment of war debts (Poole had suggested to Wilson that America cancel them as its contribution to peace and prosperity) and made no serious effort to aid the victims of European famines and epidemics; the Allies began to clamor for reparations and territory; and within a few weeks after Wilson sailed to Europe in December, 1918, Henry Cabot Lodge and his allies in the Senate were at work to undermine whatever concessions he might win from the Big Three. On September 25, 1919, Wilson's fight for ratification of the Treaty of Versailles ended when he suffered a stroke and was paralyzed;[10] but Poole had anticipated the debacle at Versailles long before the end of the conference in June, 1919.

VI Blind

His great despair over the "dismal letdown from Woodrow Wilson's great world dream" and his disgust with events at home led him to begin in April, 1919, a "war novel" entitled *Blind* which would, he hoped, open the eyes of the world to the knowledge that it had lost its "vision." The fact that he made such an attempt is a tribute to his optimism and his faith that people would respond if exposed to the truth. It also is a credit to his integrity and courage that he risked his reputation by standing up for an unpopular cause in a time of hysteria.

To present his thesis he employed the same literary form he had found successful in *The Harbor*: a fictional autobiography narrated in the first person by the main character whose purpose is to record the changes which he has observed in his lifetime and to contrast the democratic and idealistic traditions that characterized the recent past with the misguided practices of the present. By doing so, he hopes to help his readers reshape the future with wisdom and confidence. Poole transferred bodily to his main character a number of his own experiences—childhood in a wealthy family, a college education at an Eastern school, learning to write as a reporter of conditions in tuberculosis-producing slums, a flirtation with the stage, a tour of the military hospitals and cities of Germany during the Great War, and a visit to Russia in 1917. Also taken from life were characters who bear clear resemblances to the author's mother, to the Russian, Tarasov, and to his doctor friend, Harry Lorber. In addition, a number of real settings were used in considerable detail. For the remainder of the plot Poole also invented a great deal, particularly the experiences of Steve McCrea and Lucy Hart, whose careers enabled the author to widen his coverage of contemporary events and, incidentally, provide the "love story" deemed so essential by publishers. Finally, he tied the whole conglomeration together with symbolism: his narrator has been blinded both physically and spiritually by the war and, like the world itself, has to review the past in order to throw off bitterness and perceive clearly both the present and the future.

In spite of the extensive use of his own experiences, *Blind* took the author over a year and a half to complete and was not published until October 19, 1920. By that time he had regained some of his faith in progress and had exorcised at least part of his bitterness by analyzing on paper the development of his disillusionment. It is said by his son that *Blind* was always one of his father's favorite books, perhaps because writing it had brought him back from the brink of hopelessness.[11]

The plot of *Blind: A Story of These Times* centers on Larry Hart, the narrator, blinded by a German shell, who begins in April, 1919, to compose on a typewriter his life story. He is attempting a unique therapy to cure both his physical and spiritual blindness; his doctor believes that Larry is afflicted with "hysterical blindness": he cannot see because he is afraid to face the titanic problems which confront all thinking men in the troubled post-war era. Only if he can face the truth squarely will he overcome his mental block. Larry's written recollections of the past, which occupy nearly all of the novel, cover the period from 1875 to 1919 and concern the lives of three people— himself; his friend, Steve McCrea; and his cousin, Dorothy Hart —and their reactions to the disillusionments and defeats which befell them.

The narrator first tells of their happy childhood in which they absorbed the Jacksonian idealism of Amelia Hart, Larry's foster mother. Then he records the events of his college career, his futile efforts as a "muckraker" and, after he abandoned reform, his success as a popular playwright. Interwoven with his own career is that of Steve, who is first a brilliant surgeon and then, after the loss of a hand in a crippling accident, an outstanding psychiatrist. The story of Dorothy—an embittered socialist and reformer who married a German chemist and moved to Germany —completes Larry's account of events before 1914. Then he covers the characters' wartime experiences—Larry's work as a correspondent in Germany in 1914 and in Russia in 1917; Steve's service in the Red Cross; Dorothy's loss of her husband when he contracts typhus and, after her return to America, the persecution she faces because of her pacifist views. Larry concludes his survey of the past with an account of his voluntary enlistment in the American Expeditionary Force to help save democracy, his loss of sight, his discouragement with the outcome of the war, and the attempts of friends to help him recover his faith in life.

In the last pages of *Blind*, Larry reveals that writing the book has dissipated his melancholy although his sight does not return. As the narrator closes his story, he has come to accept a hopeful view of the future; the people of the world, who, in combination, would be unconquerable, will in time assert themselves; the war is only a minor setback; the people will not forget the price they paid in blood. In fact, the memory of it will accelerate the progress of their struggle against their masters. The "super patriots" in the United States will learn that necessary changes cannot be stopped by the suppression of free speech, the deportation of radicals, or the crushing of labor movements. Overseas, the Bolsheviks will also learn that their fixed creed will have to be changed and adapted to new conditions. And gradually, through the years, out of the processes of trial and error and out of the endless sacrifices of countless ordinary men, who never cease to reveal unexpected reserves of idealism and devotion, the millennium will arrive.

The length of this summary attests to the book's chief flaw: the unsuccessful attempt to cover the events of forty-five years and the experiences of many characters in a little over four hundred pages. The first quarter of the novel moves at a leisurely pace, but about the halfway mark the tempo increases steadily after the beginning of the war. So many events occur that Poole has no time to show the effect of these happenings on the people involved; he is forced to tell briefly, rather than to show, how they feel and then to move on without developing any of the dramatic possibilities. Thus the reader does not become emotionally involved with any of the characters. The impact of blindness or of losing one's hand or one's husband is lost in the flurry of occurrences. Worst of all, by the end of the book there is so little attention paid to characterization that the people become merely names instead of living personages.

A second major flaw is Poole's use of his own experiences: the material is employed clumsily and in excessive amounts. It appears that he inserted his articles on the war and the 1917 Russian revolution with a minimum of revision; as a result, the plot comes to a complete halt until this material has been covered. A reader acquainted with the author's career and his magazine publications gets the impression that *Blind* is a rather sloppy "scissors and paste" job. There is so much of the autobiographical that the reader questions whether the book is fiction or the author truly creative. Poole apparently anticipated this criticism, for the fictional author in *Blind* defends his use of real life by saying that a man's personal experiences are all he really knows of life. A more satisfactory defense of Poole's method in this book is that he knew the novel form was the best way in which to present to a wide audience his actual experiences and the conclusions he drew from them, for it is possible that only a work of fiction (or a book posing as one) could catch a sufficient number of readers for such serious material.

A third flaw is that the theme and the author's opinions overwhelm the story as they did not in *The Harbor*. The ideas are, of course, valid ones; but they occupy space out of proportion to the rather thin plot and are presented in static monologues, not dramatized. The actions of the characters and the things which happen to them are designed to illustrate the theme and often strain coincidence and credibility. The blinding of Larry, for example, is symbolism that is forced; and the sufferings of the others in the cast were obviously invented by the novelist to serve as a basis for editorial comment. It is hard to believe in the troubles of puppets, and the reader never becomes emotionally involved in their fate as he must if the novel is to make its point.

In spite of the flaws described above and notwithstanding some poor writing, a number of dull passages, and the annoying reiteration of the theme, *Blind* has redeeming qualities. The childhood experiences of Larry are as amusing and compelling as those of Billy in *The Harbor*. Later on, the complex family relationships are handled with humor, insight, and warmth. The influence of a mother on her children, the attitude of a father toward the suitor of his beloved daughter, the intimacy of brother-sister relationships, the pride and disappointments a son gives his father, the conflicts between the old and the new generation, and the shock the latter faces when it discovers that it has suddenly become the older generation—all are described with the skill displayed earlier in *His Family*. One of the best parts of *Blind* describes the delightful family machinations to bring about the wedding of Steve and Lucy, Larry's sister. Afterwards, Poole's treatment of the contrast between courtship and the everyday problems of making a successful marriage shows his increasing skill in handling one of his favorite themes. Some of the discussions of social and international problems and of possible solutions are interesting to the historian or to the student of ideas, and other passages give valuable insights into the general intellectual and emotional climate of the period, certainly no small accomplishment.

In spite of the hurried treatment, some characters remain with the reader. Aunt Amelia, although intended to be merely a symbol of an old way of life, has a distinctive personality; her philosophy and her personal charm pervade the novel, and she serves as a pleasant contrast to the unsettled "young moderns" who have neither ideals nor dreams. Dorothy is a most charming adolescent, so much so that one regrets seeing her grow up. Steve, while often a mouthpiece for ideas, at times enlivens the dialogue with sparkling and ironic comments on life; and, after he loses his hand, his efforts to overcome his disability make him particularly admirable.

Blind is perhaps somewhat more realistic than *The Harbor* in its use of profanity and sex. "Damn" and "Christ's Sake" are used frequently. Larry's actress wife is described as having a disreputable past; the reader does not, however, learn any further details. Castration, prostitutes, and the ordeal of childbirth are mentioned, matters not discussed in polite society at that time. The generous use of slang and colloquial grammar also marks this novel as one of the works taking advantage of the new freedom which became available to authors of the 1920's.

The response to *Blind* was much more favorable than it deserved. A number of the critics were willing to overlook its obvious defects in plot development, characterization, and style because the ideas which it presented were thoughtful, sane, and deserving of consideration by all readers. There were, of course, many adverse comments on Poole's excessive use of real life in a novel and on the use of fiction as a vehicle for the promulgation of doctrines, especially those allegedly of doubtful validity; and these reviews probably discouraged more than a few prospective readers. At it turned out, however, the public bought over fifteen thousand copies, either because of the novelist's high reputation as the author of *The Harbor* or because his views were reputed to be daring or subversive. It has been reported that there was even a demand for the book abroad. It was published in four or five foreign countries and even had a vogue in Germany, where it was issued as a book and then twice as a serial.[12] Poole once received a letter about it from readers in the Australian Bush.[13]

Blind, in spite of its author's determination to take optimistic views of the future of mankind, is the sort of book one would expect of a man who had more or less placed the problem of saving the world in the hands of future generations. This was, for all practical purposes, the fact in Poole's case. Never again did he throw himself completely into a campaign of reform with his former certainty that all would be as hoped.

CHAPTER 6

The Early Twenties

AFTER 1920 Poole began to devote all of his energies to his chosen career, the composition of novels. Having spent nearly two decades in the fruitless service of many causes and reform movements, he deliberately chose to live the remainder of his life for himself and his family. Yet, because he was "always interested in everything," as his friend, Otto Mallery, once declared, no significant world happenings and very few of the "fads," manners, or intellectual movements of the time escaped his attention. The books he wrote inevitably contain references to or make use of some or all of the aspects of life which intrigued him at this time. International affairs were still within his ken: he watched Russia with growing disappointment as individual freedom was abolished; in 1921 he publicly expressed his approval of the proposals for naval disarmament; and in 1923 he warned the United States of the menace he recognized in Mussolini's new Fascist state.[1] Aside from world events, the subject which interested him most at this time was the science of psychology, particularly the branch now called parapsychology, which was investigating extra-sensory phenomena in the hope of enlarging man's power over himself and his material environment.

In the early 1920's he published five novels—*Beggars' Gold* (1921), *Millions* (1922), *Danger* (1923), *The Avalanche* (1924), and *The Hunter's Moon* (1925), and a collection of sketches, *The Little Dark Man* (1925). In spite of the rapidity of production, the novels are of a surprisingly high level of conception, workmanship, and technique. Relatively little is known of the origin and background of these—indeed, of most of the works written after *Blind*—because, in the main, they are not even mentioned in the autobiography, which devotes only eighty-four pages to the years after 1920. Perhaps in 1940, when he wrote *The Bridge*, he had come to believe, as did most of the critics and the reading public as well, that he had done his most significant work in *The Harbor* and *His Family* and that there was no point in discussing any aspect of the decline of his reputation.

I Beggars' Gold

Beggars' Gold, the novel which followed *Blind* and was published on October 28, 1921, apparently was intended to dramatize one of the ideas stated at the close of its predecessor: the author's belief that the hope of the future lay in the inherent but unsuspected idealism, courage, and endurance of ordinary men and women.[2] Possibly he was stimulated to write this novel by the many examples of great sacrifice which took place during the "Red Scare," when a number of idealistic people risked their careers and reputations and usually ruined both in defending the principle of free speech. At any rate, he had no difficulty in finding true stories on which to base his plot.

The title refers to those powers in which Poole placed his faith. The expression had its origin in a remark he had heard in 1905 when a Russian compared the ignorant and poverty-stricken peasants of his rich but underdeveloped country to beggars sitting unaware on bags of gold.[3] Like those peasants, Poole said, all of the people in the world are oblivious to their own inner resources or to the fact that by using them they could bring about the arrival of a social and political millennium.

At some time during its composition, the story began to change into a novel about marriage, one of his favorite literary subjects. As he delved more deeply into the relationship of the chief characters and devoted many pages to it, the emphasis shifted from the original theme; in the finished product, the hero's defense of free speech, which occupies relatively little space, is no longer the climax of the book but a device to bring Peter to a fuller appreciation of the love and support of his wife. Even the significance of the title has changed, for the "gold" now apparently refers to the value of everyday life and marriage. As a result, it is not unusual for a modern reader, unacquainted with the "Red Scare," to overlook the original theme. Poole, himself, of course, never realized that he had almost completely subordinated his basic theme because, like many writers, he could not see his own work objectively or as a whole. This defect was not apparent to his readers in 1921, either; in their obsession with the "Red menace," they unconsciously gave greater importance to the account of Peter's "leftist sympathies" than was actually called for by the text of the book.

Beggars' Gold relates the story of the life of Peter Wells. Born in the Berkshires about 1866, he is a cautious, slow-thinking New Englander. As a youth he dreams of seeing the great and glamorous world on the outside of his village. His goal is China, but he journeys no farther than New York City, where he begins to teach in a school filled with noisy foreigners.[4] There he meets Katherine Blake, who teaches English to Chinese immigrants. Her father had given his life to the New China as an engineer, and she plans to return to this awakening world. "Like a humble elephant," Peter falls in love with his fellow teacher, in whom are combined womanly charm and the mystery of the East. They share the same dream, it seems; and to the infinite pleasure of every reader, she accepts his proposal of marriage. Their first problem is taking care of a little Chinese boy, Moon Chao, whose father was killed in a Tong war. Later, when his uncle in China sends for him, they are left alone to adjust to their life together.

Katherine, like most of Poole's good wives, understands her husband very well; and they live together with a minimum of friction. But marriage ends romance; and, for Peter, life degenerates into a wearying round of teaching and paying bills. The birth of a daughter, Susanna, weakens Katherine's heart, and she nearly dies. When an offer comes to him to teach in Peking, they do not have enough money to pay the passage for all of them. In spite of his wife's insistence, Peter will not go alone; and thus the long-awaited opportunity escapes them.

Then Peter conceives the idea of writing a biography of Theodore Roosevelt, who in 1908 symbolized the American ideal of achievement. The incredible ease of Roosevelt's rise fascinates Peter, who toils endlessly and has nothing to show for his efforts. A second opportunity to go to China comes when an uncle dies and leaves him three thousand dollars, but he still cannot afford to go because of his financial responsibilities. Instead, he uses part of his inheritance to pay his numerous debts—especially the money owed to Katherine's doctor—and quits his job while he works on his biography. He reads and labors diligently at his writing; he even has a brief interview with Roosevelt; but, in spite of all his work, Peter cannot put the living man into his pages. After he finally realizes that he has failed, he calmly lays aside his manuscript and his hopes and returns to the "daily grind."

Over the years he has been somewhat influenced by the socialists and other liberals he has met; and, although he does not join the Socialist Party, he shares their concern for their fellow men and works to bring about improvements and reforms in his school and community. By 1912 he is made a principal. His life is fast slipping away, but Peter is content. When Moon Chao, now an inspired teacher in his homeland, comes back to New York, eighteen years have passed. The couple is now middle-aged, and their child is a spirited young lady who looks with amazement upon the old-fashioned ideas of her parents. Moon Chao urges them to come to China and play a part in its awakening and its schools, but Peter does not want to give up his hard-won position as principal. Moreover, he feels too old to make the change.

Then comes World War I. Peter finds himself turning against the Germans because of their atrocities and aggression, but he is shocked to find that in America the hatred of the enemy has also been directed against pacifists and the German-born. With effort he keeps alive his conviction that out of "the Great Death" will come the world Wilson proclaimed, but his hopes are crushed by the mob violence directed at his socialist acquaintances. When they ask him to speak at a protest meeting, Peter hesitates, knowing that his career is at stake. But a lifetime of belief in the constitutional rights guaranteed all Americans—particularly freedom of speech—influences his decision. And Katherine agrees with his choice. He speaks, to little avail; and he is dismissed by the members of the Board of Education because they do not want a "Red" in a position where he can teach false doctrines to students. This sacrifice made for an ideal is the high point of a life with little of the dramatic in it. Soon afterward, Kate falls seriously ill during the influenza epidemic, and Peter faces the possibility of another great loss. At her bedside he at last discovers how important his marriage has been to him; in his relationship with his wife was a "golden treasure" that thousands of days and habit had obscured but not destroyed. After Kate recovers her health, Chao persuades his poverty-stricken old friends to make a new start with him in the New China. But their old dream of China is a small thing compared with their new awareness of the wealth which they had possessed all their lives.

Beggars' Gold, while not one of the novelist's most distinguished works, has qualities which make it one of his most moving and quietly powerful stories. The simplicity and directness of the style and the air of gentle understatement contribute greatly to this effect. Furthermore, there is no feeling of unseemly hurry as there is in *Blind,* even though this story covers a fifty-five-year period in a relatively few pages. Poole achieves this even pace in his narrative by restricting himself to the life of only one main character; he includes only those events which involve or affect him; and until the end of the story the plot is used only to characterize Peter Wells and thus prepare the reader for his act of quiet and costly heroism.

The best reason for reading *Beggars' Gold* is that it contains two of the most appealing of Poole's characters. The reader likes Peter and Kate as soon as he meets them, and further acquaintance with them deepens this affection. With the passage of time they gradually change, becoming older and sadder, less enthusiastic about life, resigned; and the reader finds himself remembering sadly the days of their youth and their comically awkward courtship, their difficulties in becoming adjusted to each other in the early part of their marriage, their mutual front in a crisis, their drift into middle age with its calmness and its "time to watch and listen," as well as its awareness of lost opportunities. In the end, when Katherine nearly dies, one shares the terrible fear which grips Peter as he suddenly realizes how important his wife is to him. Never does Poole hide the flaws in their characters—Katherine's temper and Victorian view of sex; Peter's slowness of thought and naïveté—for these traits complete the pictures of their characters and make one think of them as real people. Yet one tries (as one always does with one's friends) to overlook their weaknesses and to remember instead their quiet courage, idealism, loyalty, and selfless love for each other.

Much of the power of the novel lies in its soberingly realistic view of life. Making no concession to the public's desire for heroic actions and happy endings, Poole portrayed life as he had in *His Family;* he omitted none of the sadness, disillusions, and real defeats found in the happiest of human existences. Peter does reveal inner strength and willingness to sacrifice for an ideal, but he pays dearly for the gesture; and, ironically, there is no indication that his action makes even the slightest contribution to the cause of freedom. Similarly, the hero does learn that he has placed too little value on his work and on his marriage— but this discovery comes only when most of his life is past. Thus, Poole is saying, in this world there can be no happy endings; at best there can only be quiet ones in which the regrets are stilled but not forgotten.

World events and their implications have a place in *Beggars' Gold* as in most of the books; a reader would hardly expect one of Poole's heroes to be unaware of socialism, Debs, Roosevelt, the New China, World War I, and the Red Scare. Yet *Beggars' Gold,* like *His Family,* is almost entirely free of tiresome "messages"; instead, the author's favorite subjects are presented dramatically in the form of events affecting the characters' lives. As a result, this novel is a much better piece of propaganda than *Blind,* whose long "sermons" do not contribute to either the story or the characterization and, indeed, overwhelm the book. Only in the final pages of *Beggars' Gold* is there a lengthy and rhetorical "editorial," and, with dramatic fitness, it is delivered by an idealistic character who is affirming his belief in man's inner resources and in his consequent eventual rise to world brotherhood.

Of the two flaws in the novel, the most obvious has already been mentioned—the confusing use of two distinct meanings for the title and the presence in the book of two parallel themes, with the one which was originally secondary now receiving the greater emphasis. The other weakness is the slight attention paid to the minor characters, who, with the exception of Moon Chao and Susanna, are mere names; and even these two lack depth when they are compared with the main personages.

In spite of the small number of reviews, most of which, at best, were only mildly enthusiastic, *Beggars' Gold* sold over sixteen thousand copies. It proved to be especially popular among clergymen, several of whom asked for permission to use its rhetorical conclusion in sermons, probably without understanding the gulf between their theological views and the author's. One, impressed perhaps by the sound of the words but not clear as to their meaning, telegraphed the author for a hundred-word statement of the novel's central idea.[5] Although *Beggars' Gold* probably did not seriously enhance his reputation, it is not likely that it harmed it.

II   Millions

Poole's ninth book, a short novel entitled *Millions*, appeared on September 19, 1922. It apparently was begun after *Beggars' Gold* was finished in the preceding autumn and was written in less than a year; in fact, it was complete, except for a final polishing, by the summer of 1922, when the author started a new book, *Danger*. In later years he worked steadily on one book until he was satisfied; but in this period he often allowed the composition of his novels to "overlap" so that he could approach revision with a fresh, critical outlook.[6]

Little else has been discovered about the origin and composition of *Millions*. In all probability, he started with the idea of portraying the reactions of people when they learn that a supposedly rich relative is about to die and leave immense wealth to them. The situation gave him an opportunity to show that the hope of possessing millions brings out incredible meanness and viciousness but also, in some cases, a capacity for generosity; and it always arouses the "secret fire" of forgotten dreams. Poole saw, in other words, another opportunity to preach the lesson taught by the parable of the beggars sitting unaware on bags of gold, to illustrate his belief in a "reserve of idealism, courage, devotion and endurance, the presence of which we barely suspect, we who are so tragically blind."[7] But, at the same time, he did not hesitate to satirize man's more ignoble aspects.

This little book undoubtedly cost its author a great deal of work, for in it he attempted for the first time to produce a novel that was tightly constructed—"well-made" in the Jamesian sense. Long an admirer of Turgenev and perhaps aware of the structural weakness in most of his own books, Poole limited his action to four days—from Sunday evening to the night of Thanksgiving Thursday in November, 1921—and, with a few exceptions,

laid all of his scenes in the apartment of the dying millionaire.
He imposed on himself many of the problems faced by play-
wrights and, in overcoming them, gave his novel the virtues of
a well-wrought play. He forced himself to deal briefly and unobtrusively with antecedent action and background information.
He delineated characters by using their actions and the thoughts
they expressed in the dialogue rather than by authorial comment.
And, most important, he tried to develop conflict between the
characters at once and then work out the action in terms of
dramatic scenes rather than narrative. To unify his book further,
he used Madge, his central character, as he had used Ethel in
His Second Wife. She is the center of interest and the point of
focus; the reader sees, with very few (but annoying) exceptions,
only the events at which she is present, and much of the book is
concerned with her reactions and the portrayal of her character.
Millions is, therefore, a work displaying considerable technical
ingenuity.

The story begins on a Sunday evening when Madge Cable,
thirty-two and unmarried, arrives in New York in response to a
telegram informing her that her wealthy brother Gordon, thirty-
six, has been badly injured in an automobile accident and is
lying in a coma in his apartment. As she waits for further developments, she muses over the fact that if he dies she will in-
herit his millions and that for the first time in her life she will be a
person of consequence. Her thoughts reveal that she is puritan-
ical, in spite of her "modern" talk about sex; a man-hungry
spinster; and a failure in the eyes of her family and by her own
evaluation. Late in the evening she has two visitors in Gordon's
apartment. The first is Joe Evans, Gordon's business partner and
best friend, who impresses the imaginative woman as a marriage
prospect. He is followed shortly by a mysterious Miss Lenora
O'Brien, an actress on intimate terms with Gordon.

On Monday morning Uncle Phil Cable, the head of the family
and a former doctor, reaches New York. He makes it his business
to learn the terms of Gordon's will and then sets out to protect
Madge's inheritance from the scheming adventuress, Miss O'Brien.
He hopes that Madge will endow her town with a hospital in
which he will have an influential position. The next to arrive, at
noon, is Aunt Abby Dwight, forty-nine, the widow of a minister
and the mother of five girls. Because she was Gordon's foster-

mother, she is determined to save him from the sinful, soul-destroying clutches of the "scarlet woman." In addition, she wants to save his millions from her; for, with some justice, she believes that the money should belong to her own needy off-spring. Abby is a vivid character, a busybody armed with relig-iosity and moral clichés; but she is a good person underneath an unpleasant exterior. The tension mounts as the doctors postpone an operation on Gordon.

By noon on Tuesday, Ray, the last of the family, arrives. A cousin twenty-six years old, he is extremely crude and shallow; he is characterized by his slang and profanity and by his profi-ciency in uncovering the sins of others. He soon learns that Gordon and Lenora have been sharing the same bed on week-ends. Equipped with this information, the family self-righteously tells the girl that she is a "tramp" and refuses to let her see Gordon. Late on Tuesday evening the sick young man regains consciousness and asks to see his girl friend.

Madge now faces a dilemma. Can she permit this meeting? Her family insists that the girl is plotting to use her charms to bring about a change in the will. But Joe Evans urges Madge to let Lenora see Gordon; he argues that Madge does not under-stand the relationship between the two. When Gordon awakens again and discovers that the whole family has come, he is certain that he is dying and suffers a serious relapse. The doctor advises Madge that her brother will probably die if he does not see Lenora. Unable to decide, Madge goes to the girl; and in a long talk she discovers that the young actress is not living in luxury at Gordon's expense; she is actually working hard to keep a second-rate show on the boards. She has not married her lover because she wants to have independence and a career of her own. It appears that her sexual relationships with him have been without a selfish motive, since she really loves him. Madge is shocked by these revelations but convinced of Lenora's sincerity, and therefore she permits her to sit by Gordon's bed through the night.

So efficacious is her presence that the patient is decidedly out of danger by Thursday morning. The family, freed of its dan-gerous obsession, once again becomes a group of normal people, perhaps even admirable in its acceptance of disappointment. At this point the reader learns, as might be expected, that Gordon has no money at all and is even in debt. Nevertheless, he and Lenora decide to marry and legalize their relationship. There is even a chance that Madge will entice Joe into marrying her, but as the book closes on Thursday evening she goes to the opera alone. She is not certain of her future, but she has had her dreams reawakened. She will never return to the drifting, aimless existence she had led before coming to New York.

Millions contains some of Poole's best work, although ultimately the book leaves the reader feeling cheated and disappointed. It is a fast-moving novel—really an extended short story—and its most attractive elements are its mounting suspense, engaging dialogue, and psychological realism. Even though there are only two or three possible dénouements to the plot and it is easy to anticipate the outcome, *Millions* is for the most part entertaining reading. The trouble lies in an ending that is anticlimactic and does not provide a believable illustration of the central theme. There is only Poole's assertion that there has been a lasting metamorphosis in Madge's personality, and it is hard to see how she will go about remaking her life and overcoming the weakness ingrained by years of habit. Yet this indecisive ending is probably preferable to the conventional device of marrying the heroine to an eligible young man.

Although Poole relied almost entirely on dialogue to carry the burden of characterization, he was unusually successful. There are exceptions: Lenora, for instance, is not convincing as the high-souled mistress; Joe is a thin burlesque of the Southerner and best friend; and Gordon, offstage in a coma, receives only brief treatment. But the four country-bred relatives are as vivid as the people in *His Family*. Without mercy the novelist shows their hypocritical search for the sins of others, their lack of delicacy or manners, their feelings of inferiority and suspicion toward city people, and their fierce grasping after property. Yet he has balanced these traits with insights into their more worthy aspects. When confronted with the possibility of great wealth, they see a million dollars not as money but as an opportunity to better their lives and those of their families; and not all of their aspirations are purely selfish. They are almost admirable in their acceptance of their fate when they go home to their old lives, to existences now shabbier and dreamless, to small towns where neighbors will laugh at their brief, pathetic stand in the spotlight of wealth. Poole's determination to see the good and bad sides of his characters adds immeasurably to the depth of his portrayals.

Aunt Abby is unforgettable. She has an almost superstitious hatred of "scarlet women," and what she does not know about Gordon's sex life she creates out of a mind capable of considerable extrapolation. Typical of country people is her attitude toward the trained nurse: she treats her like a servant and refuses to let her eat with the family. Abby's religion is based on the assumption that God and Abby share the same views of terrestrial events. When Lenora is permitted to sit beside Gordon for the obvious purpose of dragging his soul down to hell and taking his money from the rightful heirs, the old lady cries out, "I wonder what God thinks of such things?"

The portrayal of Madge is completely convincing because Poole shows many flaws in her character as well as the strong points. Her constant self-dramatization and her egocentricity, which are revealed in her mental soliloquies, almost make the reader dislike her. In all of her reactions she is consistently a countrified spinster yearning for a man and yet, out of her extremely limited knowledge, conjuring up nauseating pictures of sexual relationships. She selfishly constructs a mental picture of future wealth, ease, and culture, forgetting that Gordon's life is the price for this dream world. Madge, of course, does not realize how prudish and hypocritical her views are. But she learns in time to be honest with herself; and, in the most important decision of her life, she demonstrates her basic integrity when she chooses to lose millions rather than commit a moral crime. As a result of this act, her whole life will henceforth be different: she now has confidence in her ability to make her own decisions correctly, and there is a good chance, Poole says, that she will be able to fulfill the dreams of self-improvement which the illusionary millions had awakened. Like Peter Wells and Steve McCrea, she is a failure who surprises herself by making a comeback. If the reader doubts the novelist's assertion that she will continue to be successful, it is because he has not idealized his portrait of her; a likable and deeply sincere person, Madge nevertheless lacks the drive, sophistication, and experience which are necessary to fulfill her ambitions. She has made a good start, but it is clear that the odds are against her.

Millions, like its predecessors, is set in contemporary New York and has an abundance of references to matters of current interest: Bolsheviks, European Relief under Hoover, the Red Cross, the New Woman and Suffrage, and the many changes in morals, beliefs, and standards during the post-war period. Poole was perhaps one of the first novelists to observe and comment on one of these developments—the effect of motion pictures on American ideas and ideals—when he showed that Madge had derived her ideas about love and other human relationships solely from the silver screen.

In 1922, anyone who tried to decide on the basis of the reviews whether he should read *Millions* soon found himself hopelessly confused by the extreme positions taken by the critics. One group asserted that the style, characterization, and tight organization marked an advance over Poole's earlier work and compared the novel favorably with Lewis' *Babbitt* and Cather's *One of Ours;* it was a dismal failure, said others. This group found most fault with the theme: either they believed the concept of a "moral awakening" in itself too reminiscent of "the chautauqua" or they accused the author of failing to make believable Madge's alleged spiritual growth. He was also accused of "moral earnestness" in his portrayal of Lenora O'Brien: if the author had really understood her character, it was asserted, he would not have shown her anticipating a virtuous future. E. F. Edgett, a long-time supporter of Poole, did not take sides in the argument; he later confirmed his readers' suspicions when he admitted that he had not reviewed the book because he considered it an inferior potboiler.[8] In spite of the critics' failure to arrive at a consensus, or because of it, the public decided to investigate *Millions*; and it sold over twelve thousand copies.

III Danger

Poole's next work, published on May 8, 1923, was *Danger,* a novel much more substantial in subject matter and length and certainly one of the best he ever wrote. The story of its origin and development over a two-year period is unusually interesting because, as he revealed in letters to various acquaintances, he made several drastic changes in the book before it was finished.[9] His original idea was to illustrate, as he had to some extent in books such as *His Family* and *Blind,* his conviction that since 1914 no family, not even in America, was secure from the ominous forces at work in the world. It was essential, he believed, that Americans be stirred from their complacent and unrealistic isolationism and help Europeans solve their economic and political problems before they caused a war that would again involve the United States. Therefore, he selected a cast of characters who were average middle-class Americans with lives much like those of his readers; and he devised a plot that would expose them to the repercussions of events an ocean away. As usual, he first made a general outline of the story and then assembled voluminous notes on such subjects as locale, the traits of the characters involved, the dialogue to be used in important scenes, and a host of minor details as well: "I then wrote the first draft in a fashion so rough that nobody but myself could possibly have deciphered it. From this I dictated a second draft, and during the year that followed I wrote and rewrote perhaps five or six times."[10] One of the reasons for the extensive revisions was that a new theme—the destructive power of hatred —began to occupy his thoughts.

He noticed that many of the people he met in America were still seething inwardly with bitterness toward the Germans. In Europe the French, impelled by the same emotions, were preparing to invade the Ruhr and collect by force the overdue reparations they had awarded themselves in the Versailles Treaty. Obviously, there could be no peace and no security for anyone in the world as long as the haters held the power to arouse passions that should be forgotten. He also saw clearly that hate warps and ultimately destroys those who bear it; and he seems to have sensed intuitively that these people act as they do because they are emotionally ill.

In order to put his thoughts about hatred into *Danger,* he created a character named Maud Brewer, an extreme example of the kind of person he felt all around him and whose presence increasingly frightened him. To his surprise, Maud soon began to act of her own volition, as Becky Sharp is said to have done during the writing of Thackeray's *Vanity Fair,* and her actions could not be confined to the limits of the original scheme. He became so absorbed with her personality that he decided to let her "have her way" with the book[11] and therefore discarded or changed much of what was already done. He found it necessary, for example, to concentrate on the portrayal of the other characters, who had to be made as believable as Maud and, at the same time, so buoyant and attractive that they would offset the grim mood surrounding her.[12] Most of them were entirely the author's inventions, but Aunt Eliza was apparently based on one of his favorite real-life optimists, the deeply religious, three-hundred pound great-aunt of Poole's college roommate.[13] When the book was finished, he saw that it had become the story of a marriage destroyed by a hate-driven old maid. He admitted that he had become so involved in developing his characters that he had forgotten about his theme, but he felt that the message was clearly implicit in the action: as he said, he had written "a dramatic action of real people."[14] Perhaps no other book except *The Harbor* had cost him so much labor, and seldom had he been so pleased with one of his works.

The story of *Danger* opens with Aunt Eliza Tillinghast on the morning of her eightieth birthday in October, 1920. This kind, lovable Quaker spinster serves as an observer and a commentator on events which occupy the next two years. Among her visitors on that day are her nephew, Frank Darrow, and his two grown children, Jack and Natalie. The grand-nephew is a rather brusque fellow who is both practical and impulsive. Recently returned from the war, he is now employed as an arbitrator between labor and management. Natalie at twenty-one wins the reader's affection immediately; appealing and wholesome in her attitudes, she is that rare person who is genuinely good and yet thoroughly human. She is admirably suited to represent the forces of reconstruction and positive thinking in *Danger*.

The novel is concerned primarily with Natalie's marriage to Dallas Brewer and the tragedy which comes about because not everyone could forget that the war was over. Dallas, Jack's college roommate and an old beau of Natalie's, arrives for a visit with the Darrows. He has recently recovered from a bad case of "shell shock," and it is obvious that he is not being helped by his middle-aged sister, Maud Brewer. She keeps her brother in her power by constantly reminding him of his debt to her for working during most of his youth in order to pay for his education. But, worst of all, she will not let him forget the horrors of war which brought about his breakdown. The high point of Maud's life was the war, and she is not willing to let go of it. To her the soldiers were all glorious heroes, giving their lives freely and gladly in a Great Cause. Now she devotes her time to a dozen unrehabilitated men whom she supports at her private club; she takes care of her wounded boys with the same possessiveness that she feels toward Dallas.

Natalie has no intention of marrying anyone, even though she likes Dallas; and she even rejects the proposal of Thomas Donahue, an eligible young Quaker. But when Brewer is seriously ill with pneumonia, she convinces herself and him that she does love him; and, after he recovers, they are married. At this point begins the central conflict of the novel, a struggle that keeps the reader in suspense until the very end. Natalie, who is the personification of youth, happiness, and a renewal of life and hope, finds herself opposed by Maud, the incarnation of the spirit of war and death, of hatred, vicious memories, and a distorted idealism which manifests itself in her hollow mottoes full of bitterness and destruction. Maud hates the young wife, partly because she is a rival for Dallas' affections and attention but mostly because Dallas no longer has enough money to support her soldiers' club. Consequently, she does her best to prove to her brother that Natalie is not good enough for him and that her family is interfering in his personal affairs.

The young wife watches helplessly as the demands of a neurotic and jealous spinster drive a wedge into a once-happy marriage. When she tries to defend herself, Dallas shields his sister against all arguments because he feels that he owes her a great debt. The situation worsens when the soldiers leave. Maud, who now has nowhere to live, moves into the apartment, where she torments the pregnant Natalie throughout the day and in the evenings insinuates to the husband that his spouse is unfaithful. There is only one hope of relief: Maud is planning to return to France in order to take part in that country's military chastisement of Germany for its failure to pay reparations. But the trip never materializes, and one night the vicious, deranged spinster convinces her brother that Jack has threatened her with violence; Dallas seizes a pistol, waves it at his friend, and is killed accidentally when Jack disarms him. Unfortunately, Maud is sane enough to swear out a murder charge; but at the trial her testimony, so carefully built up to implicate all of the Darrows in the crime, shows the court that she is really demented. Left to herself, she uses a pistol to end her bitter life. Jack is freed and begins to rebuild a life overshadowed by the murder of his friend; Natalie gives birth to a child, and it seems likely that she will in time marry her former suitor, Thomas Donahue.

Into this safe and happy family has come the hand of a dead war; it has almost ruined their lives. The moral is subordinate to, and implicit in, the story. It is not repeated incessantly or dragged in at odd moments for the edification of the reader. It is perfectly clear from the dramatic situation that one must forgive, forget, and rebuild.

No summary can do justice to the realism with which Poole shows the terrible effect of Maud's actions. Perhaps only those who have been forced to live in daily contact with such a person can appreciate how discomfortingly accurate the author has been. In one scene Maud walks in her sleep dreaming that she is back in a military hospital; as a result, she almost frightens Dallas into hysteria. In another episode she calls some veterans together and gets them drunk; then she parades her crippled boys before them in order to extort funds for her club. Finally, she prolongs the ordeal of Dallas' burial so that she will not have to say goodbye to him; and at the last she forces his soldier comrades to sing a stanza of "Over There." This maudlin scene is, in its own way, perhaps as horrifying as the gangster's funeral in Faulkner's *Sanctuary*. The passage describing her last moments of life is, by contrast, simple, austere, and edged with a strange kind of beauty; one is left with a feeling that Maud has found at last the freedom from her obsession and the dignity which her life of hatred had denied her.

To offset these scenes there are equally powerful ones of a different nature. Early in the novel Natalie takes stock of herself as she sits alone on the beach. She is pregnant and must face the knowledge that never again will she be a free, girlish nymph. When her little dog tries to persuade her to run and play with him, she barely notices him, so overcome is she by a dawning sense of the responsibility of adulthood. During this quiet moment of self-recognition she musters the strength for what is to come and takes the first step in what becomes a steady growth toward maturity.

This novel illustrates perhaps better than any other that Poole was a highly skilled creator of female characters; certainly he never surpassed his portrait of Maud. Not content to show her only as others saw her, or as she revealed herself in her actions and words, he often went inside her mind and followed her mental processes, either paraphrasing or quoting her thoughts for many pages. Everything she observes becomes distorted by her obsession with the war, and Poole shows how easily the devotion to a few noble ideals can become an ugly fanaticism when it refuses to admit that any other aspects of life exist or to face the fact that the world changes. Perhaps equally important, the reader comes to understand the deep roots of her problem, the terrible loneliness of an unloved human being who needs to belong and be needed, and who, having found fulfillment once, cannot find it again. In no other character (not even Grandma Barnes in *The Hunter's Moon*) did Poole create a more frightening figure of evil; in the courtroom scene, for instance, her intensity and sincerity, like that of many fanatics, almost convince the listener against his will. It is a tribute to Poole's skill that the reader also feels for her that special kind of pity reserved for truly lost souls. Maud makes *Danger* a novel that is not easy to forget.

In portraying Natalie as the heroine and protagonist, Poole faced two problems: he had to make her good without being unbelievable and he had to create a personality as strong as Maud. He solved these difficulties by having her character evolve during the course of the story. At the beginning she is a very likable but slightly frivolous girl whose life has not been touched by serious concerns. Soon she proves that she is subject to human error when she marries the wrong man. Living with Dallas proves to be nothing like her dreams, but she accepts the consequences of her folly and makes no attempt to find a way to escape. Instead, she struggles to save her marriage and her husband; as a result, she matures into a woman whose spiritual strength, courage, and will to live enable her to resist Maud's villainy to the end and, after her husband's death, to begin building a new life. The novelist wisely chose to reveal Natalie's character with a minimum of editorial comment; her traits emerge during exchanges of dialogue and in relationships with her acquaintances; in addition, other people tell their opinion of her; and, at times, the reader has access to her thoughts.

Aunt Eliza, the other important woman in *Danger*, was apparently one of Poole's favorite characters, as was the real Quaker lady on whom she was based. He idealizes the kind old woman, who has no discernible flaws; but her portrait is nevertheless vigorously alive and convincing. One long remembers her immense body and the agile mind it contains, the genteel piety, the sense of humor that includes herself, the words of wisdom she dispenses, and her quaint "thee's" and "thou's." Poole could hardly have chosen a more appropriate person to enunciate the views of the constructive thinkers who oppose Maud: she has distilled from a long life a faith in the basic goodness of mankind and an optimistic attitude toward the future; but she also knows that times of trouble are unavoidable and can only be endured.

Since the men in *Danger* occupy relatively minor roles, Poole spent much less effort in characterizing them. Nevertheless, Frank's calm strength, Jack's rough honesty, and Dallas' generous but weak personality are shown consistently and vividly. The women, however, are by far the superior portraits.

In spite of his great interest in drawing his characters, he did not neglect his plot. There are no loose ends or pointless digressions. Aunt Eliza begins and closes the book; and Donahue, the former suitor, returns in the final pages to offer a new life to the heroine. A close examination reveals the careful building of the tensions between the characters until violence is inevitable; the deaths of the Brewers come as a natural consequence of everything that had happened earlier. Their tragic exits, in turn, bear out the author's theme—that an obsession with hate is self-destructive; and, as in the Greek tragedies, the fate of the characters produces a catharsis in the reader, leaving him with a sense of completion, freedom from pain, and quiet hope.

Danger can hardly be described as "genteel realism"; one can not possibly imagine Howells treating psychotic behavior with such unsparing attention to unsavory detail. In fact, Poole himself had never ventured so close to naturalism and never did so again until he wrote *The Destroyer* at the end of the decade. One indication of the degree of realism he permitted himself is the use of profanity by women—not only by Maud but also by the heroine, Natalie—in moments of extreme frustration.

He doubtless did not worry about the fact that he would

shock his readers by being true to life in such details, but he awaited with some anxiety the response to the book.[15] He sensed that it was better than anything he had yet written, but he wanted the feeling confirmed because it was so different from his past works and had emerged from the depths of his mind without conscious effort or control. But he waited in vain for *Danger* to receive real recognition. It was not greeted with enthusiasm by the reviewers; most stated a strong dislike for the morbid theme. Yet, in spite of their objections to this supposed flaw, several critics declared that it was the first serious work of art that he had produced since *The Harbor* and *His Family*, even if it was not of their quality; and others recommended it because of its dramatic intensity and a capacity to stir the reader's emotions. After these reviews it received no further detailed attention from students of literature and since then has been completely overlooked by the literary historians.

Danger was, however, immediately successful with the public and was reprinted in May, June, and November of the same year. There was an English edition in either 1923 or 1924; and in November, 1928, it became the first of the novels since *The Harbor* and *His Family* popular enough to warrant an inexpensive edition.[16] According to Macmillan's records, the novel sold over nineteen thousand copies, a total surpassed by only four of Poole's books. But by 1937 it was out of print and subsequently was forgotten.

IV The Avalanche

Poole's next novel, *The Avalanche,* published on May 27, 1924, grew out of his interest in hypnotism, clairvoyance, and telepathy. It will be recalled that in 1917 his Russian friend, Tarasov, had introduced him to a village sorcerer whose hypnotic and "magical" powers were legendary. Finding Poole anxious to learn more, the interpreter had sent to him in America further stories about extrasensory perception and had revealed that traditionally many of the members of his own family possessed the power to follow the actions of people at great distances by means of mental "television."

Apparently Poole also had held discussions of the subject with students and visitors from India and other parts of the Orient,[17] and it is certain (judging by his references to them in *The Avalanche*) that he had a general acquaintance with the work of such men as Freud, Jung, Charcot, and Emile Coué. Part of his interest was merely normal curiosity and a reaction to the publicity which men like Coué were receiving; but he was also motivated by his psychological need to find an emotional substitute for his now-shattered faith in world socialism. In *Blind, Beggars' Gold,* and *Millions* he had affirmed that men had "deep inner resources" which were more important and more effective than any rigid and fallible "systems" of social reform; nevertheless, he still felt the need for "scientific" proof that these powers existed. Just as some men have sought spiritual strength in Catholicism, Yoga, or Zen Buddhism, so the author turned to parapsychology, perhaps the most remarkable amalgamation of the quasi-religious and pseudo-scientific ever concocted. In his defense it should be noted that he was not—and is not—alone in his hopes for the results of this new field of study, which was called simply psychology in the 1920's and was usually confused with the science which bears the name today.

It was therefore inevitable that Poole should work on a novel which would center on "psychological" aspects of man. In an interview in February, 1924, he revealed that he was writing such a novel. For the past twenty years, he said, people had been oriented to think in terms of economic determinism; but now the man in the street was interested in his inner workings and wanted to read books about the subject. He declared that in the United States the psychological novel would, in a few years, supplant fiction concerned with economic and social matters.[18] This prediction came true, for psychoanalysis soon became the subject of countless bad novels, and Marxist ideas did not return in quantity to fiction until the 1930's.

The Avalanche at first was a short story published in 1920.[19] Based on an actual happening, "The Avalanche" tells how the famous Dr. ——— from Roumania discovers that he can cure certain patients by means of his unusual psychic powers and by "suggestion to the unconscious self." He resolves to devote his whole life to the study of the workings of the human mind. But one of his patients, an advertising expert, wishes to repay the doctor by making him rich. This misguided gratitude unleashes an avalanche of publicity and a flood of neurotic rich patients.

The story, not a very good one, closes with the doctor hoping to escape his admirers and return to his work.

When Poole decided to write a novel about a psychologist and his research into the mental powers of man, he re-used the original short story plot; but he told it in greater detail and with a new set of characters. To make the situation more dramatic and to give himself enough material, he invented a secondary plot: he substituted a socially ambitious wife for the grateful business-man and further complicated the situation by including her un-successful but still hopeful former suitor. After completing his outline, he laid out his scenes, created his dialogue, and trans-ferred some of his notes on psychic phenomena to his manuscript. As he remembered it, writing *The Avalanche* was largely a mat-ter of rewriting.[20] One of the sections of his novel was drawn from notes he had made when in the spring of 1923 he talked with three Paulist Fathers in Rome, Italy, hoping to find parallels between the technique of the Catholic confessional and the methods of psychiatry. He was very proud of this material and once called the scene in which the scientist and a priest compare notes one of his best pieces.[21]

The plot of the novel concerns Dorothea "Dodo" Farragut, a twenty-six-year-old debutante and dilettante, who is engaged to Tom McKane, a hard-headed newspaperman in his forties. When Llewellyn Dorr, a promising neurologist in his early thirties, cures her of a psychosomatic illness, she is fascinated by his strange abilities. For a time she uses Dorr to arouse McKane's jealousy, but before long she falls in love with the scientist and marries him. A more perfectly mismatched couple would be hard to imagine. He wishes to continue his research in the clinic; his wife is determined to make him the most important and wealthiest man in his field by means of publicity, subtle and otherwise. Tom McKane offers the use of his newspaper, hoping that success will destroy Dorr and that Dodo will then return to him. Naturally, conflict develops rapidly between the newly-weds; Dorr attempts to continue his time-consuming and un-remunerative research, but his wife's extravagance forces him to waste his energy on rich neurotics. The conscientious man is dangerously overworked as he becomes famous and is deluged with patients. He is continually plagued by the fear that she will leave him if he fails to comply with her wishes. In the end, her stubbornness costs her the life of her unborn child, and her incredible inability to appreciate the value of Dorr's work destroys their marriage before a year has passed. Dorr's weak heart fails before his wife can divorce him, thus depriving the world of science of one of its most promising figures.

Although Poole intended to write a novel primarily "concerned with the theme of how to tap the inner resources of us all," he actually produced a work dominated by the subplot of marital incompatibility. There are two reasons for this unintentional change. First, he did not have enough material about his main theme to occupy more than a relatively few pages; even worse, that information was at best inaccurate. His knowledge of psychoanalysis was chiefly derived from books of doubtful merit; and when he ventured into the realm of parapsychology, he relied on even shakier sources. After forty years of advancement in psychiatry and dissemination of information about the science, even a casual moviegoer today knows more about the subject than Poole did then; therefore today's reader finds his descriptions unconvincing. Second, he failed to make his scientist vivid or forceful enough to dominate the novel with his personality and his ideas about psychiatry. Instead, Dodo becomes the central figure and proceeds to draw attention to her efforts to make her husband fit into her schemes of personal aggrandizement. Thus, *The Avalanche* becomes another of the stories of married life and its problems rather than one about psychiatry.

Unfortunately, even the auxiliary plot fails to capture sustained interest because Poole's handling of his favorite theme is, for once, tedious and unrewarding. Dodo is almost the only character who inspires belief, and she is so detestable that the reader has no sympathy for her. The portrayal of this hard, shallow, obstinate, and selfish social climber occupies the first half of the book and is a convincing one. But Poole then spends the rest of the novel spinning out further instances of her self-conscious posing, plotting, and self-righteous rationalizing. As a result, the inevitability of Dorr's destruction becomes increasingly clearer; and there can be no surprises or climactic moment for the weary reader who stumbles with Dorr through many dull and unnecessary pages. The author, furthermore, gives the details of Dodo's plots in narrative form; he should have condensed the action of his story into well-planned scenes, as he had done in earlier books.

Too often the style of the novel is marred by mannerisms, clichés, and triteness. Tom always addresses Dodo as "old girl," and she calls Dorr her "dear boy." Such expressions as "flew into his arms," "deep and dreamless sleep," and "desperately in love" are used frequently. And once again the title word is repeated unnecessarily to remind the reader of the subject of the book.

There are, however, at least two passages which are effective. One is an account of a traumatic experience of Dorr's childhood. It begins when the lonely, overly imaginative child, who had been lying awake inventing elves and other creatures to amuse himself, creates a bear and frightens himself into hysterics. His mother, a scientist and a materialist in philosophy, soothes him and tells him not to be afraid since there is nothing in the darkness. However, the comfort is short-lived; later that night he sees her walking in her sleep, crying out hopelessly into the empty darkness into which her dead husband has gone. The child's fear of the monster is made truly frightening, but the agony in the mind of his mother is even more tellingly presented. Similarly, Dorr's death is deeply moving. Unlike his mother, he has come to believe that there is a life beyond death, and his last conscious awareness, like that of the hero of *His Family*, is of a great burst of light and the unshakable conviction that there is no death.

The critics were correct in calling the novel a failure. As they said, Poole had attempted to take advantage of a current public enthusiasm and had failed to deal convincingly with a highly uncertain subject. A second major weakness was his inability to make the characters seem real. Moreover, he had tried to do too much. One reviewer wondered whether *The Avalanche* was a satire on society and its concept of success, an examination of modern marriage, a tract on faith healing, a study of neurology, or a clash of the ideals of Coué and the Rockefeller Institute. The answer is that it was all of these with none of them adequately subordinated to a central theme.

Nevertheless, the fact that Poole mentioned the novel in *The Bridge* indicates that in 1940 it was still one of his favorites;

indeed, *The Avalanche* is still considered by his personal friends to be one of his most memorable books. With the public it was popular; over thirteen thousand copies were sold, but there was no reprint as a "paperback." Some of the sales can perhaps be attributed to the interest in Coué; for a time nearly everyone in America hoped that "every day in every way he was growing better and better" because of autosuggestion.

V   *Collection of Short Stories*

A collection of short pieces, *The Little Dark Man and Other Russian Sketches,* was published on April 21, 1925, and may be thought of as a kind of companion volume to *The Avalanche,* since it deals with a similar theme, and to *The Village,* because of its content. During his stay in Russia in 1917, Poole became interested in the proverbs, songs, and imaginative fables of the peasants; he was especially attracted to tales of the mysterious powers possessed by gifted human beings. Poole, stimulated by their underlying theme of extrasensory abilities, reworked these tales while he was composing *The Avalanche*; and he published some of them in the *Atlantic, Harper's,* the *Independent,* and *Our World.* Soon after their magazine appearance they were collected and issued as *The Little Dark Man and Other Russian Sketches.*

This book is divided into four sections. "The Dormeuse" and "The Little Dark Man" are tales of supernatural occurrences; they contain several memorable characters, are fairly well organized, and proceed effectively, in spite of their leisurely pace, to their dramatic conclusions. "Stories That His Uncle Told" is a loose collection of anecdotes in which the humor of the peasant, rather than the supernatural, predominates, and "Mother Volga" consists of legends about Russian saints and other mythical personages. In these two latter sections are some delightful anecdotes and fascinating glimpses into the mind of the Russian peasant. Unfortunately, they are unified only by their narrators; most of the material is dull and trivial, and that which is not loses its effectiveness because it is treated too casually and too briefly. The book is, in the final analysis, merely a collection of magazine pieces of varying interest and not a considerable contribution either to ethnology or literature.

His own attitude toward the supernatural and extrasensory occurrences in these stories is ambiguous. He wished to believe in the existence of strange powers beyond the ken of science; during the war, he had seen in the willingness of men to die for an ideal and in the ability of strong spirits to overcome bodily infirmity and disaster proof that awesome powers (which, for lack of a better term, he called God[22]) actually existed in the hearts and minds of human beings. But apparently he was too much a believer in demonstrable facts to accept hearsay evidence or folk stories as irrefutable truth. At any rate, he treats the tales as interesting material rather than as illustrations of man's occult powers. It is perhaps better that he did not pursue the supernatural elements too far and contented himself with using these tales as a way of giving a realistic portrayal of the peasant mind.

The reviewers of *The Little Dark Man* were as sharply divided as those who wrote about *Millions,* but in this case an unusually high proportion of the notices—nearly half—were partially or wholly unfavorable. Poole was accused of taking advantage of the vogue in Russian materials to "palm off" on the public a collection of commonplace stories, few of which transmitted the spirit of the Slavic nation. Even Tarasov's accent (which Poole, a master at recording speech characteristics, had faithfully reproduced) was regarded as fake.

The publishers lost money on this venture, partly because of the reviews, partly because it is much more difficult to sell a book of short pieces than a novel. The public bought only fifteen hundred copies—the worst reception of any of the author's books. His Russian friend Tarasov also fared poorly, for Poole had arranged to share the proceeds with the penniless exile. There were, however, profits from the original sale of the pieces to magazines and a royalty from the reprinting of "The Little Dark Man" in an anthology. This story, by the way, had been recommended to the editor by Poole as an example of his best work.[23]

VI *Commonplace Realism*

The abysmal failure of *The Little Dark Man* confirmed in the minds of many critics what some of them had been saying for years: Poole had "written himself out" in his first major novel. The impact of *The Harbor* had been so great that they felt cheated when he did not turn out another of epic proportions but, instead, with the exception of *Blind,* concerned himself with novels (and often novelettes) limited in scope to the personal problems of a few characters. Even *The Avalanche,* which had promised a theme of vast significance, was in reality merely another study of the problems of modern marriage. His refusal to return to such topics as class warfare was to critics a sign of decreasing creative vitality and an increasingly barren imagination.

Of course, the truth was that he had turned to other themes out of choice, not necessity; he believed that one could discover the same great truths about mankind and society by examining the family—the microcosm—that one could find in a survey of the total social structure. Indeed, only by limiting one's scope and examining the individual could one really show the inner working of human nature. In short, he had become a realist of the commonplace determined to show accurately how ordinary middle-class people lived, thought, and reacted to their problems. Undoubtedly some of his critics and readers were willing to accept novels of this sort; certainly many had found *His Family* superior to *The Harbor.* But many of these supporters had not been pleased by the successors of the Pulitzer Prize winner, some of which, like *His Second Wife* and *Millions,* they dismissed as "potboilers." Refusing to acknowledge the brilliance of *Danger,* they lamented more and more that his magic had faded.[24] His performance in his thirteenth book, *The Hunter's Moon,* admittedly did nothing to change their minds.

VII   The Hunter's Moon

Practically nothing is known of the genesis of this novelette, a story concerned with the rescue of a lonely little boy from a hostile environment, an unhappy home in a big city. Poole doubtless knew of many situations in which children were caught between warring family factions; it is known that he worked hard to enable New York children to escape from the sweltering city for a few weeks in summer camps, and from these experiences may have come his inspiration. His decision to tell part of the story from a child's point of view may be traced to his reading Edwin August Bjorkman's *The Soul of a Child* (1922); in a letter to Bjorkman he stated that, until he had read his book,

he had felt that adults could only "romanticize" children and
their thoughts; Bjorkman had now proved that the real mind of a
child could be presented convincingly.[25] It is evident that Poole
resolved to duplicate this feat. His little novel appeared on
September 8, 1925, with a cover design by Abram, his prize-
winning artist brother. More a short story than any of the
previous novelettes, it was padded to a respectable length by
large type, empty pages, and illustrations.

The central character of *The Hunter's Moon* is an imaginative
nine-year-old, Amory Barnes. His trouble actually begins ten
years before the story opens when Ruth Wade, who likes music
and pretty clothes, marries Frank Barnes. Her mother-in-law
hates Ruth from the start because she likes to spend money on
things the older woman considers valueless. Frank's mother has
raised herself from poverty by constant hard work and endless
economizing, and in the process she has become obsessed with
money. She believes that her wasteful daughter-in-law is drain-
ing Frank's small wages and preventing him from gaining financial success. Therefore, she begins a ten-year conspiracy to get
rid of Ruth; by moving in with the couple, nagging, criticizing,
and finally by cleverly and falsely accusing Ruth of adultery,
she undermines the marriage of the young people. Ruth is willing
to leave with her child but finds that Grandmother Barnes is
determined to rear him to be a practical businessman. To escape
the constant quarreling in his home, Amory takes refuge on the
roof of the tenement, where he plays games by himself.

This background is sketched in quickly as the story opens with
the arrival of Grandfather Wade. An easy-going world traveler
who makes a living by collecting folk songs, he is determined
that the little boy will be allowed to grow up normally in the
free life of the countryside. To the disgust of Mrs. Barnes, he
stimulates the "romantic foolishness" of Amory with the stories
he has collected on his journeys. Although he hopes to rescue
both Ruth and Amory, he finds that he and Ruth cannot take the
child with them: he is convinced that the old woman could win
custody of Amory by showing her "evidence" of the mother's
infidelity. Although apparently defeated, the old idealist predicts that Amory will be so unhappy in the barren world of
Grandmother Barnes that she will soon gladly return him to his
mother. After his mother leaves, the boy does become so heart-

sick and lonely that in a few weeks his grandmother sets him free; and another small boy escapes the dirty city and a dreamless future of pointless drudgery.

The outstanding accomplishment in *The Hunter's Moon* is the characterization of the grandmother. Poole made her so vivid that she overshadows all the other characters. Everyone is ineffectual in the face of her vicious and singleminded schemes, her meanness, and her spitefulness; only a person equally purposeful could hope to defeat her on her own terms—and no such character exists in the tale. Her decision to move in with the newlyweds is fiendishly clever and typical of her machinations; from the moment she rudely awakens everyone by loudly closing the windows until the last grim meal is finished, she pursues her goal. In spite of her heartlessness, Poole is fair to her and explains that she was warped early in life by fear of poverty and by the loss of all but one of her children. She hopes that Amory will be a substitute for her lost babies; but, for all her possessiveness, her groping for affection, and her grasping, she will never get what she wants; and she will never know why. In a sense she is to be pitied rather than despised.

Many parts of *The Hunter's Moon* can be described as excellent reporting of the facts of life. The unsavory family quarrels and the scene in which Ruth is accused of adultery are painfully lifelike; the hurt that comes to children cursed with unhappy homes is searingly delineated. The treatment of sex is realistic but restrained; for instance, Ruth's longing for sexual satisfaction is mentioned but not exploited for the purposes of sensationalism. Furthermore, profanity is seldom used by the characters, probably because it would not have been typical of them.

In general, *The Hunter's Moon* is stylistically on a very high level. With experience, hard work, and long practice Poole had evolved a style which was clear and direct and, in spite of its simplicity, strong and effective. But his handling of technical problems was not equally successful. Apparently he intended originally to write a "well-made" novel, as he had done in the case of *Millions*; his plan was to limit the action to a short period of time, to use as few locales as possible, and to unify the book by concentrating on Amory's actions, observations, and thoughts. This intention was carried out in part and then abandoned; the resulting impression is that Poole had apparently decided that the technical devices were not worth the trouble.

The time scheme, for instance, is strictly adhered to through three-quarters of the book. The story begins on the evening when Grandfather Wade arrives; using the expository techniques he had learned as a playwright, Poole reveals in dialogue and Amory's memories the events of the preceding ten years; then he presents a series of scenes which culminate on the next evening in the departure of Ruth and her father. In addition, all the action up to this point has been confined to the flat, to the tenement roof above, and, in the afternoon, to a beach. Then, after this display of technical prowess, the novelist suddenly discards his dramatic method and his unity of time and space and hurriedly summarizes the happenings of the next two weeks. As a result, the reader, who had anticipated a dramatic scene showing the defeat of Mrs. Barnes, feels cheated. He may even suspect that Poole, having created an indestructible villain, was unable to bring off a convincing ending and therefore took the only alternative.

Equally disappointing is his use of Amory as an observer. The little boy is not supposed to understand the significance of all he sees and hears, but at times his lack of comprehension is almost moronic; yet on other occasions he manifests insights that are so perceptive as to be unbelievable. The final indignity visited upon the reader is that Poole, after beginning with Amory, soon switches to the third-person omniscient or to the minds of the other characters. Obviously *The Hunter's Moon* would have been greatly improved by the use throughout of the objective point of view. It is clear that the artistic example of Henry James meant nothing to Poole; if it had, it might have prevented him from publishing this technical fiasco.

It is indeed surprising that, with one exception, the reviewers found much to commend in a book which all admitted was at best "slight" and which was "charming" rather than significant. The point on which the critics were divided was whether the presentation of Amory's mind was a success. Several spoke with praise of Poole's ability to interpret a boy's mind and delineate his psychological outlook, but an almost equal number found the child very strange or simply unreal. There was also criticism of the shifting in point of view, which, it was felt, only served to confuse the characterization.

A book with a few scenes of searing realism and one unforgettable character, but far too many weaknesses, *The Hunter's Moon* was not destined for immortality. Nevertheless, it sold nearly eight thousand copies and, according to William Poole, would have done even better if the public had not been misled by its cover into thinking that it was a story for children. Poole's reputation would have been better served if no one had bought and read this latest effort; such books as *The Hunter's Moon* helped convince the public that his best work had been done.

CHAPTER 7

The Late 1920's

DURING THE REMAINING YEARS of the 1920's, Poole continued his orderly production of prose despite the continuing decline of his popularity. His output included three novels, *With Eastern Eyes, Silent Storms, The Destroyer;* a book-length biography, "Captain Dollar"; a "novel" composed of loosely linked short stories, *The Car of Croesus;* and nearly forty magazine stories and articles. And this listing does not include many manuscripts which his literary agents were unable to sell. The quality of this material is extremely uneven: *With Eastern Eyes* and *The Destroyer* are unquestionably his best work in the novel form; and, with a few notable exceptions, the magazine stories are his most inferior work in any form.

I With Eastern Eyes

With Eastern Eyes, which appeared on October 13, 1926, is a novel of little more than two hundred pages. In spite of the fact that it is perhaps his most nearly perfect work, Poole made no mention of it in *The Bridge* or elsewhere in his published works, an omission which indicates that he considered it of little consequence. This theory is substantiated by his letter to Lillian Wald dated a day after the book's official publication; in it he thanked her for her favorable reaction to an unnamed novel (undoubtedly a complimentary advance copy of *With Eastern Eyes*) and described it as merely a "between books" effort; but he added that it was one on which he had expended much labor. It had been finished before he had gone abroad in March, 1926, and had begun work on a long novel about the new forces stirring in Europe (*Silent Storms*), a subject, he implied, that really merited his attention.[1]

It is not surprising, then, that little can be learned about the origin and development of *With Eastern Eyes*. The records of Brandt and Brandt, his literary agents from 1924 to 1929, list in 1925 a story entitled "With Eastern Eyes," but it was never sold and the manuscript has vanished. It is possible that, like "The Avalanche," this story was a first attempt at a subject which later became a novel; but, of course, this is conjecture. The only discoverable parallel between Poole's life and the events in the book is found in a reference to a winter evening in 1925 or 1926 when the Pooles learned that one of their sons was ill in a school near Boston; but, because of a storm, they could not learn any details and spent long hours in worry.[2] A similar incident in *With Eastern Eyes* is one of the turning points in the plot. The unanswerable dilemma is, therefore, whether Poole's line of creative thinking began with the real incident and grew into a novel or whether he simply fitted it into an already developed idea.

The general sources of the book can, however, be deduced with some accuracy. The central theme, the difference in the points of view of a New Englander and a Russian, came from the author's experience in Russia; in fact, the character Pavel Boganoff bears a close resemblance to Tarasov, who was also the model for characters in *Blind* and *The Car of Croesus*. A second theme, the problems of marital readjustment which come at age forty, was derived from observation and also from personal experience: in his forties, he, like his characters, had been forced to accept the fact that his children were almost adults and that he was no longer young. The hero's wife, Jo, like Katherine in *Beggars' Gold* and Ann in *The Destroyer,* has many of the traits the author admired in his mother and his own wife. For a locale he used New Hampshire, his adopted home for many years; it is possible that an astronomical observatory he describes was based on a real one in that area. Finally, it is not surprising to find extensive knowledge of the latest theories of the stargazers in a novel written by a man who was curious about many things, particularly about science. Although these are the general materials he worked with, it is difficult to find in them the spark of inspiration which welded them into a piece of writing unprecedented in the writer's canon for economy, singleness of effect, and depth of characterization.

In the plot of *With Eastern Eyes*, Pavel Boganoff, a Russian astronomer, arrives in September, 1924, at the New Hampshire home and observatory of Bertram Dana. He has heard of the scientist's work with astral photography and has come to America to assist him with his research. Boganoff finds it difficult to understand a family of typical New Englanders who conceal or suppress their emotions; in Russia, he recalls, people talked over their problems for hours with any who would listen. A kindly philosophizer who is long on speculation and short on action, he sees everything with his "eastern eyes"; he acts, therefore, as a commentator on the events which follow.

The Danas have made a success of their lives during twenty years of marriage. Bert, aided by his wife's money, has built his own observatory and has become well known in his field. Jo, given emotional security by the love and companionship of her husband, has overcome her childhood fear of loneliness and death, has established a happy family, and has successfully encouraged their four children to be mature individuals. But now the Danas find that they must adjust their lives to a new situation—the last of the children are leaving home. The youngest boy, Jaspar, is being sent to school at Exeter, and Ann will soon be married. Jaspar does not want to go to school, preferring to stay with his father and to become an astronomer. Although Jo does not wish to see her last child leave home, she forces herself to do what is best for him. For this reason she is angered when both Boganoff and Bert try to change her mind.

Boganoff's interference has an unhappy result: the husband is forcibly reminded in front of a stranger that Jo holds the balance of power in the household. Soon afterward, the marriage of Ann forces upon Bert the realization that he is no longer a young man; but, like most men, he refuses to put aside his delusions; instead, he begins to look for ways to assert his belief that his virility is undiminished. Both Jo and Boganoff sense the restless state of his mind, but the wife is very angry when the Russian, trying to help these people he admires, gives her a veiled warning about Winifred Hubbard, a vivacious divorcée who lives nearby. Emotionally adrift, Bert begins to respond to this young woman who seems to offer both a relationship in which he will be the dominant personality and proof that he is still a young and desirable mate.

Although Jo is increasingly plagued by fits of jealousy, she is too inhibited by her New England upbringing and too proud to admit her feelings to her husband and to discuss the matter with him. In fact, she further alienates herself from Bert by acting toward him with increasing coldness; and the result is that Winifred accomplishes the seduction on a winter evening in January. When Jo comes to the observatory and finds that Bert is missing, she realizes from Pavel's behavior that the worst has happened. Her world crumbles; she is torn by jealousy and sickening hurt; and, as she looks up at the cold indifferent stars, she feels again the terror of being alone and unloved. Her first impulse is to exact revenge. She has recently been made financially independent by a substantial share of her father's fortune, and she reflects grimly that, without her, Bert will be penniless and will regret as long as he lives that he betrayed her love and repudiated his great debt to her.

For the third time Boganoff interferes: he tells the distraught wife the Russian folk story of how the universe began as a puff of God's breath on a cold morning. He assures her that her problems are nothing when seen in the perspective of eternity and that if she looks up at the stars she will find consolation in the smallness of her anxiety. In spite of his eloquence Jo is not converted to his point of view—in fact, she hardly hears him; as the minutes pass, she regains her composure and makes an awesomely mature decision: she must swallow her pride and salvage as much as possible from her marriage. She realizes that revenge on Bert, although momentarily satisfying and richly deserved, will inevitably also harm her and the children. She realizes that without her husband and her preoccupation with household routine she will find herself left alone to face the terror of death and the vast nothingness that hangs between the stars. Furthermore, she has responsibilities to the children: Jaspar will be returning home from school in June, and Ann will need her parents when she comes home to have her first child. Even Bert still needs her; without her approval and encouragement, he will not complete his life's work. Thus, when Bert confesses and prepares to take his due punishment, Jo forgives him. She cannot do otherwise; yet she will never be able to forget the pain of the betrayal; and, therefore, in her practical way she resolves that in the future she will not permit Bert to be exposed to temptation.

She has learned her lesson, and she will never again allow pride to threaten the world she has built.

With Eastern Eyes is a novel in which character portrayal is the dominant element; the action is largely concerned with psychological reactions and inner conflicts. For this reason a judgment about the success or failure of the book must be based primarily on the effectiveness of the presentation of the characters. It is quite possible that in this novel Poole surpassed all his previous achievements.

Because Jo is the central character, he spared no pains in portraying and motivating her. As a result, she is the most clearly realized character in *With Eastern Eyes*—indeed, in any of his novels. Jo is a warm and passionate wife, intelligent and well-informed, and an excellent mother. But she has a normal share of pride and more reticence about expressing her feelings than is good for her. More important is the nagging memory of a traumatic experience she had undergone as a small girl when her mother died. She had suddenly realized that the stars were not flowers in the fields of heaven; that they were only distant spots of light moving in unending dead emptiness; and that, in fact, there was no heaven, no life after death. Jo never regained her religious faith; and, because a person cannot live a life that is meaningless, she began over the years to construct a little world—a family of her own—in which she was needed and which gave her a purpose and an anodyne. Thus she is vulnerable: the loss or estrangement of her family would mean a return to the nightmare of a universe dominated by cold and death. Because the reader has been made to understand the precariousness of her psychological balance, her almost obsessive need to mother Bert and the children, his sympathies are entirely with her. And, in the end, when Jo faces the truth about herself and forgives her husband because she has no other choice, the portrait is completed in a way that is logical, inevitable, and full of insight into the nature of human drives and motivations.

Bert, too, is carefully presented because his inner conflicts precipitate the crisis. This portrayal is accomplished by scenes which bring out his childish pride in his athletic ability, his sensitivity concerning his wife's money and dominance, his inability to face middle age with sufficient emotional maturity. But Poole also gave him other traits in order to make him a complex human being. He is a very attractive and personable host; a warm, impetuous lover; a good father; and, in spite of his reckless and boyish youthfulness, a patient, hardheaded scientist.

Another well-drawn character, Pavel Boganoff, serves as both a commentator and an active—though minor—participant. Like the impractical Russian liberal on whom he was based, he is a starry-eyed incompetent. His efforts to prevent disaster only bring new tensions, and in the climactic scene the heroine pays no attention to his bland philosophizing. But, ironically, she is saved from self-destruction by the very duration of his unconsoling narrative. One cannot help admiring the ingenuity of this use of a catalytic character and the clever manner in which Poole avoids the obvious. The way he arrived at this unusual conception appears to be that Boganoff, like Maud in *Danger*, came to life during the composition of the novel and proved to be so unlike his blueprint that the story underwent a drastic shift in emphasis. Although nothing is known of the evolution of the novel, its title suggests that in the author's original scheme the Russian was intended to play a major role and to save Jo's marriage with his story about the Creation. Such a person of course would need to be an astute psychologist who could take decisive action. It seems likely that in the course of reworking his original plan Poole found that Boganoff was unexpectedly coming to life as a bungler and that Jo was becoming the main figure and a person who could shape her own destiny; the Russian thus was no longer really necessary to the plot but was so delightful and gave such a wry ending to the tale that he was retained. If this is what happened, *With Eastern Eyes* was definitely improved by these changes.

Winifred Hubbard is the least convincing of all the people in *With Eastern Eyes*. At times she is only a type, the "gay divorcée"; but Poole gives enough insight into her psychological nature to make her come alive, to reveal how frighteningly shallow and selfish she really is. She moves toward the seduction of Bert in a manner which is almost blind and unmotivated; she has no real physical desire for him, but adultery offers her a new experience. In her last note to Bert she thanks him for a lovely night and announces her departure; although she had promised to deliver a brand of love more stirring than Jo's wifely affection, she proved to be interested only in spending one evening with her conquest. She never stops to think what her actions will do to the wife. Self-indulgent, clever, and spoiled, a woman who takes all and gives nothing, she is a perfect foil for the heroine.

Even the minor characters of *With Eastern Eyes* are carefully set before the reader. Jaspar is an entertaining adolescent, and Jo's father is a colorful old scoundrel whose profanity is as picturesque as his adventures on the stock market. The reader closes *With Eastern Eyes* with the conviction that the characterizations in this book are the best the author ever did.

Moreover, the story is a masterpiece of organization and arrangement of material. Unity is achieved in two ways: first, by using Boganoff to open and close the book and take part in the crucial events, and, most important, by having him comment on the characters and happenings. The second and more important method is the centering of the story on Jo after the introductory pages: she appears in almost all the scenes; and the reader is concerned primarily with her thoughts and reactions. Poole's care in organization is illustrated by the fact that there are no elements that are superfluous or without relevance to the story. For example, early in the narrative Ann, Helen, the youngest daughter, and Jaspar talk with Jo about their future plans. These three short scenes characterize the children; show Jo as the mother, planner, and chief power in the household; reveal that for the first time all the children will be away from home that winter; and establish at least two strong reasons which prevent Jo from leaving Bert in the end. By making scenes like these serve a number of purposes Poole managed to say more about life and people in two hundred pages than he usually managed to say in two novels of greater length. It should be noted also that the time limit is carefully defined; the story runs from September, 1924, to the second week in January, 1925; but its slow and relaxed pace enables Poole to enrich the novel with details about the people and the times, to infuse humor and philosophical comment, to show man in his relationship to his own times and to the starry and infinite universe.

With Eastern Eyes represents the writer at his stylistic best—clear, deceptively simple, with none of his favorite mannerisms, the repeated theme word and the magniloquent conclusion. As early as *His Family* he had demonstrated his ability to compose lifelike dialogue, and this novel illustrates how much better he had become at the task. Pages of stimulating conversation on a variety of topics move the action forward and unobtrusively sketch in the personalities of those talking. For example, the lines given to Jaspar and Jo's father could not be spoken by any other character because the author has written their voices and peculiar outlook into their every word.

The title indicates that the original theme was the contrast between Americans who were so concerned with action that they never had time for thought and the Russians whose drive lost itself in perpetual Hamlet-like speculations. But, as usual, the author found his favorite theme—the problems of marriage in an average middle-class family—attracting his best efforts away from the thesis of the novel. The element most likely to remain with the reader is the study of the adjustments which face a couple who discover that they have reached middle age and their spiritual menopause. In this situation one either tries to turn back, like Bert, or accepts the inevitable and moves ahead, as Jo does. As in the case of Natalie in *Danger*, the decision to face reality is a brave one, and it brings with it the chill of loneliness because the marriage partner does not make the transition.

Another theme is the effect of a sin or crime, such as adultery, on the innocent victim. The handling is remarkably like Hawthorne's in *The Scarlet Letter*, even if Roger Chillingworth and Jo Dana do make diametrically opposite choices. If one seeks revenge, he destroys himself; if he forgives, he saves his own soul. Because Jo chooses the more difficult role and is willing that she alone suffer, she effectively prevents the evil from having further repercussions and makes it possible for her whole family to live untouched. This is only one of the author's treatments of the subject of adultery, but it remains his best, in spite of the power of the theme in *The Destroyer*.

The reviews of *With Eastern Eyes* are few in number and unduly brief. The critics found the book acceptable and worth reading, a definite improvement over the esoteric *Avalanche*; but it was, they said, a rather inconsequential work, especially for the man who had written *The Harbor* and *His Family*. It is clear from their comments that they did not consider a book to be "of consequence" unless it had epic proportions, adventure with a rapid pace, romantic characters, and a dramatic ending. Evidently, the 1920's had little use for the "genteel realism" Howells had advocated. At any rate, not a single reviewer recognized the fact that the novel was Poole's writing at its best.

The book sold only a little over six thousand copies. According to two sources, it received a better reception abroad than at home and ran as a serial in France.[3] This fact, however, had no discernible effect on the reputation of the novel at home; there is no basis for the statement in the *Literary History of the United States* that *With Eastern Eyes* is one of the books for which Poole is remembered.[4]

II Silent Storms

Poole's next book, *Silent Storms*, issued on October 4, 1927, fared somewhat better. It might be described as his contribution to the "international novel" because the plot concerns the marriage of an American to a French girl and shows the effect of two disparate cultures on their relationships. On this level, the novel belongs to the tradition established by Henry James; but in actuality the story is a vehicle for the author's interpretation of the current world politics, in which he had once again begun to take a serious interest. *Silent Storms* thus fits more accurately into the same category as *The Harbor* and *Blind*.

The novel grew out of Poole's observations of conditions in Europe during his frequent visits and particularly while he attended sessions of the League of Nations in Geneva as a correspondent. He saw danger in the fact that in 1926, while the United States was experiencing an unprecedented economic boom, many countries in Europe were facing financial ruin—a situation which the American public viewed with an indifference born of ignorance. Many of Europe's citizens began to agitate for dictatorships which would bring internal stability and thus benefit business and stimulate capital investments. Simultaneously, the communists were using the poverty of the lower classes as a pawn in their game—the incitement of a revolution of the proletariat. Separating the European nations and preventing them from helping each other were barriers of hatred, distrust, and tariffs. However, if they disliked one another, they loathed the United States, the creditor of the world, which they openly criticized as materialistic and lacking in culture.

Unfortunately, in 1926 the American people were tired of Europe's troubles and its snobbishness. They wanted back the money they had loaned the Allies and favored a return to isolationism. Ernest Poole was one of a little group of men who realized that a financial withdrawal would instantaneously bankrupt Europe, wipe out faltering democratic regimes, and start a new series of wars that inevitably would involve the United States. Therefore, in order to awaken America to the danger it faced, he presented this new international crisis in a novel in order to reach the largest possible audience. He used the marriage of an American banker and a poor French countess as an allegory of the American-European situation; neither makes any attempt to understand the other, and the partnership ends in dismal failure. The moral seems to be that a marriage of naturally incompatible people cannot succeed unless both sides compromise and make an attempt at understanding. Poole hoped that statesmen, backed by an alert electorate and public opinion, would apply this same formula to world problems and quell the silent storms of bitterness and strife. In brief, then, *Silent Storms* is a novel of purpose in which the author used his favorite formula: a story of the problems of marriage combined with a dramatization of his analyses of current events.

According to his own account, he spent nearly three years in thinking over the subject before doing any writing; then the actual composition took about nine months. Begun in France in the summer of 1926, it was finished late in the winter of 1926-27 in New Hampshire.[5] An acute observer of American upper middle-class society, Poole undoubtedly knew of a number of transatlantic alliances on which to base his story, and there is some reason to believe that the rich middle-aged banker and his young impecunious bride were modeled on a real couple. The analysis of the international situation was formulated from firsthand information and observation; the author had visited Paris and Provence (where part of the story takes place) on several occasions, had written articles about the Fascist dictatorship in Italy, and had reported on major developments in the League of Nations at Geneva.[6] European hostility to America was obvious in the newspapers, and he undoubtedly picked up some of his anecdotes about "dollar diplomacy" from his numerous acquaintances in New York. The treatment of Wall Street is based on actual experience, for references to broker friends occur frequently in *The Bridge*.[7]

Silent Storms covers the period from September, 1924, to the early months of 1926, a period especially selected for its turbulence and diplomatic crises, many of which are treated in the novel. Barry McClurg, who possesses the most dissonant name of any of Poole's characters, represents a striking departure from his usual main character: McClurg is an international banker, a Republican, and a staunch conservative with the viewpoint of a George Babbitt or an unreconstructed Silas Lapham. In short, McClurg stands for almost everything the writer did not.

At forty-eight, Barry is comfortably settled for life. He enjoys his work in foreign investments and has an understanding companion in Charlotte, the mother of his long-dead wife. Since the two are also almost exactly the same age, he wishes to marry her; but the woman prefers not to become the wife of her son-in-law. In spite of her strong influence, Charlotte is unable to prevent McClurg's marriage to Madeleine de Gronier, a beautiful young French countess with no money and with positive Fascist leanings. Madeleine, fascinated by the power Barry wields, sees him as one of the world rulers in a near future when governments of politicians are to be replaced by boards of enlightened financiers. In this and other respects she greatly resembles Poole's plotting heroines in *His Second Wife* and *The Avalanche*, and she is no more appealing than her predecessors.

The chief obstacles to their marital adjustment are the differences in their ages and their aims. Barry is deeply involved in his work, which, of course, is too esoteric for his wife. Also, he hopes to convert his flighty mate into the mother of a family and the mistress of the mansion he wishes to build. Madeleine, on the other hand, finds domesticity very dull and the company of young friends her own age a necessity; she has no desire to have children or a home—she is a "modern" woman. Whenever she finds his passion too boorish for her fastidious tastes, she locks the door of her room. She also uses his position to further the activities of her Fascist friends.

The issue which creates the biggest rift concerns her plan to settle in Paris; only in her homeland can she obtain that culture which she claims is an essential part of her life. McClurg, naturally, cannot leave New York, for that city is the center of the world of finance; nevertheless, he agrees to visit her family home in Provence. He is not impressed by the "tradition" behind the unsanitary old chateau, and he is not overjoyed at the reception her parents give him. These members of a dead nobility have that indefinable and non-negotiable abstraction, "culture," and little else. They want money and hate the Americans who give it to them; they resist any progressivism in French politics and back reactionary Fascists in the hope of regaining power. Hurt by their rudeness and convinced that European tradition and culture are a farce in the modern world, Barry returns to the United States. The imminent birth of a child offers momentarily the hope that the marriage will survive. Even so, the father learns to his sorrow that his offspring must become a Roman Catholic. But this problem is solved neatly by Madeleine, who refuses to obey the orders of her doctor and, as a result, gives birth to a dead child. With nothing to hold them together, the couple now agree on a Paris divorce. At the end of this two-year period of excitement, Barry returns gratefully to the quieting companionship of Charlotte. His experience, however, has given him a deeper insight into the outlook of Europeans; and, at the end of the novel, he advocates to his colleagues a more liberal financial policy in foreign investment.

Silent Storms is a thoroughly unsatisfactory book. For one thing, there is very little humor to alleviate the sordid theme. The novel is also entirely too long, and one very soon becomes weary of the thin "love" story. But the chief flaw is that only three of the characters are ever more than names, and these three fail to engage the reader's sympathies—a tragic weakness in any book. Only Charlotte has genuineness and depth, but she is not quite understandable or believable. Barry is so dull, plodding, and unimaginative that one can appreciate Madeleine's restlessness. But the reader's dislike of women of her type—stubborn, shallow, petty, selfish, incapable of passion or abiding love—is so strong that one finds her husband more likable because he is at least generous, stable, and honest.

Another major weakness is that Poole seldom shapes his plot into dramatic scenes; he simply recounts the events in narrative form instead of showing his characters talking or acting. The very few dialogues are dull and lifeless, except when Charlotte is present, and too often they take the form of endless monologues on the world situation. Furthermore, the various attempts to include contemporary matters and discussions of world events are very awkwardly inserted into the plot, which at best is weak. As a result, the action is at a standstill for many pages. Even the characters are all too obviously moved by the demands of the allegory which insists that they constantly misunderstand each other and produce in the end a dead baby, just as in world politics the misunderstanding of Europe and America will produce nothing of value. Poole's original theses were, in most cases, fairly well subordinated to the study of the problems in marriage by the time he finished writing a book; unfortunately in this one his original idea retained its pristine vigor and resulted in a mechanical and unrewarding work.

The chief value of *Silent Storms* for the purposes of this study is its record of Poole's thoughts in 1926 on the crucial state of the problems of the nations. It was his first thorough review of his ideas since *Blind* in 1920, and time has proved that his analysis was, in general, correct. But his preoccupation with such matters resulted in a plot which was patently an allegory and in characters who were only personifications.

And yet the majority of the reviewers were enthusiastic over *Silent Storms*, which several described as Poole's best work to date and far superior to *His Family* and *The Avalanche*. There was little support for the critic who dismissed *Silent Storms* as "a rather thin and tedious story" inspired by a wistful memory of *The Harbor*. An indication of the level of competence of the reviewers, however, is that one of them made the statement that Poole, who was identified as a political conservative and an advocate of Big Business, wrote in the style of Upton Sinclair at his worst but without Sinclair's social consciousness.

The praise awarded this book now seems amazing, but the total sale—over eighteen thousand copies—is almost unbelievable. As late as July, 1931, the demand was still sufficient to warrant a seventy-five cent reprint from Grosset. Only three other books by Poole have been, to date, reprinted in popular editions: *The Harbor, His Family*, and *Danger*. The only possible explanation would seem to be either the presence in the book of characters based on persons recently involved in a scandal or else the public's predilection for poor books. In any case, it was the last of his works of fiction to become a popular success.[8]

III *"Captain Dollar"*

Poole's next work that warrants consideration here was a serialized biography of Captain Robert Dollar, a shipping magnate whom he once admiringly described as "one of the last of our pioneers." By 1928 his fame was such that the *Saturday Evening Post* commissioned Poole to prepare a book-length study. Early in the summer of 1928 he and his wife were on their way to the West Coast to collect material. Acquaintances of Dollar proved to be most cooperative, and the old man himself was an excellent source. Poole spent many days following him as he went about his astounding round of activities, took down his flow of anecdotes and comments on a variety of topics, and occasionally cornered him in his office for more formal interviews. The length of the direct quotations in the published work indicates that Poole had forgotten little of the techniques of reporting he had learned on the East Side of New York.

Born in Scotland in 1844, Dollar moved to Canada at the age of fourteen; in fifteen years he had worked his way up from lumber camp chore boy to lumber baron. In 1893 he bought his first ocean-going steamer; and by 1902 he was trading all over the Orient. During World War I he served on the board that drew up the Emergency Shipping Bill and then further helped the war effort by selling or leasing (at considerable profit to himself) many of his ships. After the Armistice he rebuilt his fleet by buying at a nominal price a number of the steamers which the Shipping Board had obtained at exorbitant rates. Seven of these ships were employed in Dollar's most ambitious, daring, and successful scheme—around-the-world passenger and freight service with a liner leaving the West Coast every two weeks. Thus it was that an eighty-year-old man climaxed a remarkable career with a display of business acumen that put to shame men half his age.

"Captain Dollar," which appeared in the *Post* during May and June, 1929, undoubtedly satisfied the editors and the readers.

The abundance of factual matter is presented in clear and simple prose and is enlivened by numerous anecdotes. In certain instances the long direct quotations which preserve the idiomatic flavor of the various speakers make the reading especially entertaining. At times the narrative itself, particularly the accounts of life and suffering in lumber camps or adventurous escapades with Chinese warlords, is as fascinating as a good historical novel. And from the work emerges a clearly etched portrait of Dollar.

But when "Captain Dollar" is judged by more stringent standards, the weaknesses become evident; it is only a competent piece of hack writing. Among the flaws is the principle of organization: instead of presenting his material in a strict chronological order, Poole usually preserved intact the rather discursive interviews and tried to maintain a sense of unity by inserting them within the thin framework of his own experiences while interviewing. The method inevitably results in repetition and in far too many dull passages. The style, too, is not Poole's best. Often the reader feels that he merely set down notes without revision and grew bored with his recitation of facts. The work as a whole, in spite of some unforgettable passages, suffers from dullness and intolerable length—although this aspect is probably exaggerated by the eye-straining type and format used in the *Post*.

But perhaps the most serious flaw is the complete absence of criticism of Dollar's ideals and methods. Nowhere is there the suggestion that his methods in lumbering (which destroyed countless redwoods and irreplaceable forest areas) were reprehensible or that his opportunism and profiteering in wartime were capitalism at its worst. There is not even a hint that there is something incongruous in the Bible-quoting habits of a strict Presbyterian who crushed unions with calmness and carried Chinese coolies in his ships as if they were cattle. Of course, the blame for this omission cannot be placed wholly on the author: had such criticisms of Dollar been presented, the editors would have removed them—to retain the advertising of the Dollar Line and to avoid an uproar from success-worshipping readers. The fact remains, however, that by an ironic turn of events, Poole in 1928 found himself emulating the career of Billy in *The Harbor* who in 1910 was turning an easy dollar by flattering capitalists in his magazine biographies. It is little wonder, therefore, that the few remaining socialists like Upton Sinclair believed that Poole had joined the enemy.[9]

In spite of the weak points "Captain Dollar" is perhaps better than most magazine biographies; therefore, one may wonder why the work never received publication in book form; the answer apparently is that such a venture, which might have been subsidized by the publicity men of the Dollar Line, died in the cold dawn of the Great Depression. On May 16, 1932, Dollar himself died; his great dream soon followed him into eternity; for, in spite of the best efforts of his son, there was no business to be had, and in 1938 the United States government seized the Dollar Line's ships when he defaulted on a $7,500,000 federal loan with which the vessels had been purchased.[10]

For Poole, too, the coming of the Depression was a grim fact. Although he had predicted a day of reckoning when the insatiable greed, folly, and materialism of his fellow Americans would have to be paid for, he was not really prepared for the Crash of 1929 and the aftermath. He himself had made thousands of dollars in paper profits in a three-month period after he had placed nearly half of his funds in an investment trust: suddenly this capital was gone, along with its customary regular earnings. During the late 1920's over half of his large income had been derived from his writings; only a small part was the royalties on his novels: the rest came from generous editors of such periodicals as *Redbook, Cosmopolitan,* and *Collier's,* who paid as much as a dollar a word for pieces that are for the most part of unbelievable sorriness. Now that market and the easy money had vanished forever.

For Poole, a new and austere way of life had begun. Ever mindful of others, he intensified his efforts to help the Salvation Army and YMCA obtain funds to feed the unemployed in the Bowery breadlines; but there was little he could do for those many Americans who were bankrupt—particularly those who had lived for a decade without any ideals or aspirations except those of the market place. For Poole, his own course was clear: in the hope of making some money he hurriedly assembled a little book for his publishers.

IV   The Car of Croesus

On March 25, 1930, was issued this product of necessity, *The Car of Croesus*, supposedly a short novel but actually seven short stories loosely connected by an introduction, conclusion, and the appearance of the two central characters in every story. Four of these tales and the general introduction had earlier appeared in the *Ladies' Home Journal*. It is possible that the *Journal* originally had intended to publish the full series, but then dropped the idea and printed only the best of the collection. At any rate, he added three more stories and a conclusion to the magazine version and made extensive revisions, particularly in "The Fairy Tale of Benjamin." Obviously, he tried to improve the stories, which he may have felt were of little value; but these alterations are confined to wording and do not significantly alter the triviality of the original pieces.

The framework for these stories is a fantastic scheme conceived by an exiled Russian prince, who resembles Tarasov, and a pretty American who has worked as a clothing buyer for a Midwest firm. They put all their money into a fabulously ornate Rolls-Royce and rent it for a hundred dollars an hour to New Yorkers who wish to make an impression with this visible symbol of wealth. In addition to the financial return, the couple expect, by a judicious use of a mirror and a concealed microphone, to learn for their own amusement the life stories of their passengers. In the end the schemers are married; and, taking their Rolls-Royce, they sail for Europe.

The Car of Croesus is nearly the worst book Poole ever wrote. He had often contributed low-caliber stories to magazines in the late 1920's, but seldom had he allowed these ephemeral pieces to be published in book form. Clearly he now felt the pinch of the Depression in both his pocketbook and his artistic conscience. The plots of these stories remind one of O. Henry's lesser Arabian Nights' tales. They are incredibly artificial and devoid of truth or interest. The characterization in almost every case is non-existent; the Russian is a pale copy of Pavel Boganoff of *With Eastern Eyes* and a ridiculous caricature of Poole's friend. Memorable moments are few. In one, the prince manages to amuse the reader when he courts the American girl and lewdly informs her that she needs a good husband every night, a role he will gladly fill. In the first adventure there is a very colorful gangster named Chester, who gives assurance in his extravagant manner, "We won't let the crimson tide flow if we can help it." Also amusing is the plea of the young bride in the same story; she wants her husband to "go straight"—in other words, to pay for police protection instead of hijacking the liquor trucks of his friends. With the exception of this tale, the stories in *The Car of Croesus* are sentimental, boring, and free of reality, poetry, and thoughts of any consequence. It is no surprise therefore that the reviewers expressed the opinion that the book was unworthy of the man who wrote *The Harbor*. Its style was compared to that of *The Rover Boys;* its stories were described as, at best, light entertainment, and, with exceptions, "too silly for serious consideration." Less than six thousand copies were sold to a cautious and depression-ridden world, a total which apparently included the English edition.

V   The Destroyer

Unlike its predecessor, *The Destroyer,* published on September 29, 1931, is one of Poole's best novels; but, as in the case of *With Eastern Eyes*, nothing is said about it in *The Bridge*. Written during the period following the Crash, it was naturally concerned with his gloomy thoughts about the tragic pageant of the 1920's; however, he wisely decided to deal with only one of its saddening aspects—the young satirical or naturalistic writer who at first did good work but ultimately was destroyed spiritually by his own destructive point of view. There is reason to believe that he had in mind one of his own acquaintances, Sinclair Lewis, who was famous for his bitter cynicism and for the savagery of his attacks, but a man in whom Poole saw the frustrated idealist who wanted a better world.[11] The book also gave Poole an opportunity to criticize the opportunism of some of the younger writers who, he felt, were taking advantage of the current public fascination with sordid events, vulgarity, and vicarious disillusionment. Eugene O'Neill, he hinted, was quite willing to make a fortune out of the gloom and scandal in such plays as *Desire Under the Elms*,[12] and he once referred to F. Scott Fitzgerald as one of the "hell-raisers" of the period—

obviously not a compliment to the author of stories about the "sad young men."

Inherent in *The Destroyer* were, of course, his views of what materials could legitimately be used in a novel. Having long fought against censorship of his own work and being a member of the Committee for the Suppression of Irresponsible Censorship,[13] Poole was a firm advocate of freedom of expression and choice of subject matter—if the material could be justified on artistic grounds, and the content were "true-to-life," and the author's outlook were "constructive" (if he showed what man was and what he might become). Even though he had a wide acquaintance with much of the ugliness of existence, he, like Howells and Booth Tarkington, believed that a "true" account of life had to be representative and balanced; one which dealt with only the extremes of human experience and character was, at best, a half-truth or a distortion. For this reason he preferred works like Willa Cather's *My Ántonia*, Tarkington's *The Midlanders*, the novels of Zona Gale, and Lewis' early books, *The Trail of the Hawk* and *The Job*.[14]

There was, of course, a place for the works of naturalists and satirists. Poole recognized the truth in their unrepresentative pictures of the dark side of American life and their denunciations of the "surface evils" in contemporary life; he agreed that exposure of evil, folly, and hypocrisy was necessary;[15] but he demanded that it give way to a balanced perspective and constructive commentary—or at least to a consideration of the deeper, universal human tragedies. Poole saw, if others did not, that the fashionable naturalists seldom achieved their goal; either they needlessly touched youth with "the wand of despair" or they merely satisfied the public's longing for cheap thrills. Thus they often did much more damage than they dreamed possible; frequently, they themselves were plunged into deep disillusion, desperate lives, mental crack-ups, and suicide.[16]

The proof of the sincerity of Poole's belief is seen in his steady refusal to use sordid material for its own sake. His friends, alarmed over his declining popularity in the 1920's, often urged him to choose material which would appeal to the public taste. Although he undoubtedly could have widened his audience by doing so, he rejected the idea—perhaps out of the stubborn conviction that he was right, perhaps because he was constitutionally incapable of pessimism. It is therefore ironical that in *The Destroyer*, in which he attacked naturalism and gloomy writers, he produced his most nearly naturalistic work—a relentlessly grim picture of human moral decay, one whose constructive message never interferes with the tragic flow of events or the author's display of one of his keenest and most depressing insights into human nature. Nevertheless, *The Destroyer* does not violate any part of Poole's doctrine: in fact, it illustrates how liberal it was—and, more important, that adhering to it did not prevent one from writing a powerful novel.

The Destroyer, like Poole's other books, drew upon real life for some of its material. For instance, it gave him a chance to record his observations of the lives of the new generation. Into this book he poured all he had seen of a group that lived without faith, danced to jazz, violated every ethical code in search of a thrill, reached its sordid end in institutions and breadlines, and only occasionally found personal salvation. Indeed, the details of the last days of the hero of *The Destroyer* were drawn from scenes Poole had observed when he had visited the New York Bowery after the Depression had begun. When he decided to make his hero a dramatist, the material about plays, playwriting, and the theater came, of course, from his own experiences in that field. The character of Jack's mother, like most of Poole's good women, was patterned possibly on his own wife or was an idealization of his mother. Jack, the hero, bears some resemblance to Sinclair Lewis, whose career apparently inspired Poole to write the novel; but he is in fact a composite of a number of writers, including perhaps Fitzgerald and even Poole himself, whose disillusionments in 1920 were written into the fictional character.

The Destroyer deals with the life of a young idealist whose bitterness against the society of the 1920's ruins his life. Jack Wyckoff returns disillusioned from the war and the tragedy of Versailles to face a more personal blow: Leonie Marquand, his college sweetheart, is about to wed Jack's own brother, Blair, a very successful banker. To Jack, who has disliked his brother from childhood, it is obvious that Leonie has betrayed her love for him in favor of financial security and luxury. He is certain that he is physically more attractive than Blair, and thus his male pride is hurt. Although Jack declares repeatedly that his sub-

sequent actions are aimed at the hypocrisy and materialism of
the times and are generated by his own ability to see the truth,
Poole makes it obvious that his real motive is much less noble
than his alleged one. Tennyson once suffered a similar hurt; his
sublimated emotions culminated in a vision of man's glorious
potentialities in the poem "Locksley Hall." But Jack's resentment
is turned against mankind; and in a short time his plays, written
in ever stronger acid, make his fortune. The first of them, a
musical revue, mocks advertising and Prohibition; the second,
The Wild Cat, "a simple, crude, and very thin story," uses gang-
sters to show that men and women are soulless animals; the third,
The Prostitute, with obvious references to Blair and Leonie,
lashes at the female parasites who are wives only in a legal sense.
Jack skims the scum off the 1920's and throws it in the face of the
public. In return, this public makes him rich by attending his
plays to hear the off-color lines—but to overlook the satire.

Under the delusion that he is becoming more honest and
truthful with each successive play, Jack has actually been digging
his own psychic grave: in time he will believe in nothing.
Recognizing this danger, his mother, Ann Wyckoff, urges him to
look at life as a whole. A representative of Poole's own idealistic
generation, she sees faith in good as essential to happiness. Her
own successful marriage has taught her that people can achieve
ideals if they are willing to think in a positive fashion. But her
talks with Jack are in vain; each time that he hurts her with
cynical bitter words, he sinks deeper into nihilism. His point of
no return arrives dramatically when his mother learns that she
has a malignant cancer and gambles on an operation rather than
see her perfect marriage decay as she dies painfully and slowly.
In her last talk with Jack, she pleads with the wayward son to
renounce his cynicism, but he cannot bend his satanic pride to
please the one person whose praise he most desires. When she
dies soon after the operation, he feels that his refusal cost her the
will to live; thus guilt further complicates his inner turmoil, and
the decline of the once laughing, brilliant satirist is rapid. His
wit becomes a sullen sneer, his critical detachment a limitation
of vision and lack of perspective.

Drink, a debasing affair with Ginny McLane, an actress of
low repute, and finally the seduction of his brother's wife complete his self-destruction. Jack, who had often bragged of his

prowess as a lover, learns abruptly that Leonie is not shaken to the depths by his passion; she finds adultery cheap, disgusting—and uninteresting. Deprived of the one delusion on which his egoism has been built and with Leonie's taunts ringing in his ears, Jack stumbles out of her hotel into the tempest of the world now shattered by the Depression. He goes into a theater, and, as he sits in the audience watching one of his productions, he sees about him enjoying the play the very people whom he had hoped to sear with his pen. Overwhelmed with guilt and self-pity, he goes to the Bowery and the breadlines, drinks "smoke" (a poisonous distillation of wood alcohol), and contracts pneumonia. At thirty-four, weary with abnegation, and at long last aware of his own shallowness, he dies with the heart-breaking Byronic comment, "I thought for just a night or two that life was a tragedy—but it's not. . . . It's only a farce. . . ." In six years the idealist who had set out to destroy the hypocrisies of his time has destroyed himself.

In all, *The Destroyer* is a very depressing book—but one of Poole's best. The culminating passages are as forceful, compelling, and unforgettable as the climax of *The Harbor*. The effectiveness of the prose is not limited to the conclusion: the dialogue is surpassed only by that in *With Eastern Eyes*. The story progresses by means of a series of brilliant, witty conversations; and each scene fills in the character portraits at the same time that it enables Poole to present in a seemingly artless manner the points of view and philosophies of life of salient characters. For instance, the confrontations of Ann and her husband, Billy Wyckoff, serve to underline the strong, warm affection between them and to show by comparison the shallowness of the "love" of the younger generation. The talk between Homer Gale, Ann's embittered father, and Jack contrasts the latter's gay attack on surface evils with the old man's knowledge of what he ironically calls "the grand perennial jokes of God." And, as has been suggested, the basic conflict of the ideals of the two generations comes to light when Ann tries to save her son from himself. In these scenes, more than in any others, the reader sees Jack's piecemeal disintegration when he deliberately hurts his mother as he himself has been hurt by the realities of life. The emptiness and futility of his sex-ridden society are established by the way Jack talks to his young women and by their responses;

with them, he is crude and vulgar with his innuendoes and propositions. These bright young people specialize in cynical aphorisms like "the wages of sin are good cold cash." "If God made him in his image, then God must be a funny old bird," says Ginny McLane. "We're no good unless we can laugh," decides the hero as he gives his last advice to his mistress, though he can barely breathe. Even the quotations from Jack's musical revue are memorable; Uncle Sam's Prohibition agents sing: "We are bastards, one and all—and we're here to wreck your business —with our bastard little law." Unquestionably, it is the dialogue— the talk full of sparkling repartee, hard-boiled cynicism and idealistic insights, bitter quarrels and affectionate love, and wide- ly different views of life—that gives *The Destroyer* its power to convince and move the reader.

In spite of the realistic and scintillating dialogue, *The Destroyer* would have failed if the characters, and particularly Jack, had not been well delineated and properly motivated. Of course, he reveals himself in his speeches and his actions, but the reader also learns what other characters feel about him and, in addition, sees both his flaws and virtues when Blair is introduced as a foil. As a result, the author does not need to editorialize about his chief actor.

The portrayal of Jack is eminently successful, perhaps Poole's most skilled presentation of a male figure; and it demonstrates that the novelist completely understood the complex forces and emo- tions which can turn an idealist into an embittered cynic capable only of self-destruction. He shows that, in part, Jack is a victim of the shallow, materialistic society against which he revolts and that he suffers from the occupational disease of the satirist: in time, he can see only evil and baseness in his fellow men and eventually loses even the last illusion of a satirist—his belief that ridicule will change the world. But Jack's spiritual disintegration also grows out of the ugly side of his own personality; it is clear to everyone except himself that his attacks on society are really attempts to avenge himself on his brother and the woman who hurt his ego. Furthermore, his own immoral and dissolute pur- suits are motivated by the hopelessly adolescent desire to attract Leonie's attention and make her realize that she is responsible for his discarding of his former principles of behavior. Yet in the final reckoning, Jack is destroyed, not by his bad traits, but by

his best ones—his honesty and his idealistic view of life. After he
has seduced Leonie, he suddenly sees himself as a hypocrite and
therefore much worse than the people he has attacked. Unlike
the amoral and calculating Leonie, he cannot live with himself
after his terrible moment of self-discovery. Thus, despite all of
his failings, Jack remains essentially an admirable person.

The supporting characters are also fully realized people. Ann
Wyckoff, witty, warm, strong, and earnestly trying to save Jack,
fills the novel with her personality and leaves it ringingly empty
after she dies. Through her, one better understands her son, for
her choice of a brave death rather than a cowardly life reveals
the moral character which Jack inherited and which made him,
too, renounce a cowardly and meaningless existence.

Billy, a rather cynical surgeon, occupies a philosophical position between Ann's and Jack's. A doctor often knows the seamy
side of life better than others do, and Billy is no exception. But
he has seen people live on will power alone, and he knows that
there is an inexplicable power in the human spirit. But in the end
he cannot find any faith or consolation when both Ann and Jack
die tragically.

Leonie, like Winifred Hubbard of *With Eastern Eyes*, is
shallow and calculating. If Jack had not idealized her, if he had
applied his critical judgment to this woman as he did to everyone else, he would have seen the truth. Leonie is witty and attractive, but she possesses endless resources of selfishness. She
leads Jack on to see what he will do; she is simply curious. When
she discovers Jack's intention to tell Blair of their affair, she
needlessly and mercilessly destroys his ego and his pride in order
to protect herself. Leonie is frighteningly real.

The minor characters are adequately developed but seldom
vivid. Blair is merely a foil to Jack and a colorless one, perhaps
because he has only a small part in the story and rarely appears.
Ann's father, however, is more impressive. It is he who sets the
mood of tragic foreboding which dominates the story. For some
reason he reminds one of Melville in his old age—tired, waiting
for death, angry with God.

The Destroyer represents Poole's furthest venturing away from
"genteel realism" toward the sordid realism characteristic of
many writers of the 1920's. The dialogue, for instance, is often
marked by crudeness, vulgarity, and profanity. Yet the use is

easily defended as typical of the characters using it and stressing the emotional impact of climactic situations; on one occasion Poole himself as narrator uses profanity for emphasis. The material also bears a close resemblance to that of the naturalists: Jack's death is as ugly and grim as any in Dreiser, while subjects like abortion, adultery, free love, and alcoholism are discussed openly. It should be noted, however, that Poole observed certain limits: for instance, he refrained from giving physical details of the brief bedroom scene between Jack and Leonie. Thus the selection of material illustrated his message to younger writers: one should not hesitate to use the matter of the naturalists if it serves a valid, artistic purpose, but sensation for its own sake is meaningless.

It seems incredible that such a powerful and effective book should have been scorned or overlooked by literary critics, but that is what happened. Several reviewers obviously subscribed to the theory that Poole's ability had declined since the publication of *The Harbor* and, therefore, closing their eyes to the facts, declared that *The Destroyer* was further proof of his lack of creative ability. A number of critics, it appears, assumed in advance that the story was another example of the postwar cynicism of the "Lost Generation" and completely missed the fact that Poole was attacking the views held by Jack. As a result, their complaints about the author's nihilistic views are absurd. Of the available notices, only one showed any real understanding of the author's aim. The general public was equally obtuse: there were only two printings, and the total sales barely exceeded four thousand copies. Apparently not even a change in subject matter could help stem the decline of Poole's reputation.

CHAPTER 8

The Years of the Great Depression

THE STOCK MARKET CRASH of 1929 was only the beginning of America's economic crisis. As the situation worsened, an estimated four million Americans were reduced to the status of paupers; and still there was no sign of permanent economic improvement even during the early years of the New Deal. Although Poole was in no danger of real poverty, feeling in need of money for the first time in his life was an unpleasant experience, especially after years of enjoying a high standard of living. He also suffered a strong feeling of guilt because he had lost the funds which he had hoped to pass on to his children in order to make them financially independent as he had been. Furthermore, he deeply regretted his inability to help those in the breadlines in the cities and on the unfruitful farms of New England. Above all, he dreaded the possibility that free enterprise and democracy would be replaced by a Fascist or communist police state like those in Europe. It is no wonder then that the effects of financial losses on people of his social level are employed frequently as the central issues in much of his fiction in this period.

The 1930's were the most unproductive and discouraging years in Poole's literary career. His publications were few—a short book of non-fiction (*Nurses on Horseback* [1931]), two novels (*Great Winds* and *One of Us* [1933, 1934]), slightly more than a dozen articles and short stories, and, finally, after years of silence, an autobiography (*The Bridge* [1940]). The reception of the two novels was not enthusiastic; a third, which never saw print, was rejected by several publishers; his reputation sank so low that it became practically non-existent; and, exhausted by years of labor and disheartened by failure to equal the success of *The Harbor,* he gave up the novel form as a lost cause, and, it appears, even abandoned regular working habits. During the 1940's he again took up steady composition, but nearly a dozen years passed (1936 to 1948) before he tried his hand at book-length fiction once more.

I Nurses on Horseback

Nurses on Horseback, the first of Poole's books to appear in the 1930's, originated in one of his many efforts at fund-raising for the needy. In May, 1925, Mary Breckenridge, a descendant of a noted Virginia family, a licensed midwife, and a social worker, had begun the Frontier Nursing Service in the mountains of Kentucky—a greatly needed project. By 1932 the Frontier Nursing Service had grown from three to thirty-two nurses, had eight thousand people under its care, and served fifteen thousand in various ways. Although the primary work of the nurses was midwifery, they naturally assumed the general care of families and launched campaigns for disease prevention. As a result, they soon began to eliminate the epidemics, the hookworms, and the suspicion of the independent but unenlightened backwoodsmen. But this work took money. Mary Breckenridge obtained funds by making appeals to the public and publicizing her work with tours, speeches, and personal appearances. Then from the winter of 1930 until April, 1931, a drought and the Great Depression created a critical situation: relief work had to be added to the Service's duties; but, since the whole nation was in economic trouble, few had money to contribute.

Among those without cash was Poole, who therefore decided to help in the publicity campaign. For several weeks in November, 1931, he spent many hours on horseback following the nurses on their rounds through almost impassable trails and observing their selfless efforts to bring new lives into a better world. As he took notes and photographs, he became deeply impressed. The careless courage and untiring work of these dedicated nurses, the practical plans of Mary Breckenridge and the visible signs of accomplishments, and, above all, the strength and innate worth of the mountain people themselves inspired him as few things had done since his own campaign against tuberculosis in the slums and his coverage of the 1905 Russian Revolution. He declared enthusiastically, "I loved that job. It was such a relief to be writing about people who cared so little for money and whose lives were still so close to the very elementals of things." In June, 1932, *Good Housekeeping* published "The Nurse on Horseback."[1] He then enlarged his article by using his abundant notes and published the extended version as a book, *Nurses on Horseback*.

Even today this little book catches the reader's interest and fires his sympathies and imagination. It is one of those rare pieces of "muckraking" which have survived the alleviation of the conditions that inspired them. Poole had lost none of the ability, learned as a reporter, to get people to talk, to select anecdotes which were dramatic and of human interest, and to combine these bits with statistics which would arouse the reader to action in support of reform. In good journalistic fashion, the book opens with a dramatic night call for a nurse, who gallops off to aid a woman who is "punishin' mighty bad" in childbirth. He follows this scene with startling statistics: the U. S. has lost more women in childbirth than men in all its wars. Then an appeal is made to one's patriotic instincts: America needs the kind of men who come from the grass roots; if this experiment is successful, it will help lay the groundwork for similar projects on the "other old frontiers." He then illustrates the characteristics of these proud people to prove that they are worth saving: they will shoot to defend their rights; they love their children; they will starve before they will beg; they need help only to be able to help themselves. For the factually inclined, the author includes clear, concise accounts of the nursing centers; the long preparation required of the nurses; and the cost of the medical care. Thus he used every possible device for capturing potential philanthropists.

Scattered throughout the volume are numerous anecdotes and human interest stories; little character sketches, complete with the vernacular of the area; vivid pictures of people, homes, and superstitions; authentic tales of unselfish heroism on the part of the nurses; and even an analysis of possible methods for relieving regional poverty—a prediction of the Tennessee Valley Authority. It is these aspects of the volume which keep the reader interested even in dry statistics and which still make the book worth reading. Unquestionably, nothing Poole ever wrote is as effective as his brief descriptions of childbirth under primitive conditions, of women who remain heroically silent throughout, on occasion, "long crucifixions ending in death." Nothing is more appealing than the picture of the bright future the little children will have if education and health services are adequate. *Nurses on Horseback* is a good piece of reporting, but it owes its power to the fact that the writer was overwhelmed by the silent enthusiasm of the nurses, by this visible affirmation of the power of man's inner resources.

The reviewers were impressed by the social message of the book and the excellent descriptions of Kentucky mountaineers. A number of them affirmed that they were interested in further-ing the work of the Frontier Nurses. Almost without exception, they praised the qualities of the hill people, their genuineness and lack of affectation, their courage and pioneer spirit, their neighborliness and self-dependence. In short, they were so con-vinced of the value of the nurses' work that they reiterated the writer's main points for those who might not see the book.

The first printing of *Nurses on Horseback*, which appeared on September 6, 1932, sold so well that the Macmillan Company found it necessary to run off additional copies six times in the next twelve years and sold in all nearly eight thousand copies; no book by Poole except *The Harbor* was reprinted so often.[32] Because librarians often recommend it to young people interested in nursing and because its relative shortness makes it the ideal book for student nurses who have required reading, *Nurses on Horseback*, although out of print, is perhaps Poole's most widely read book. It will undoubtedly continue to hold this position in the future, but because the name of the author means nothing to these readers, his literary reputation will not be affected.

II Great Winds

The Great Depression was in its fourth year when Poole brought out *Great Winds* on May 16, 1933. It was a matter of course that the man who had analyzed contemporary events in *The Harbor*, *Blind*, and *Silent Storms* should write a novel about the most significant event of the times. During the early days of the New Deal, Poole, unable to resist the impulse to be as close as possible to the scene of important events, spent much of his time in Wash-ington observing the frantic experimentation of the new govern-ment. He found himself in sympathy with those who were trying to salvage order from the chaos and, like the majority of Americans, was thrilled by the ringing declamations of President Roosevelt. Though he approved of the New Deal schemes for social security and protection of the aged, he was surprisingly unsympathetic with other innovations. The changes, he feared, were too fast, the nostrums too theoretic and inadequately tested, the cost of the deficit spending a burden the nation could never sustain. Apparently, he found the theories either too difficult to comprehend or too dull to hold his interest. In the end he rejected the works of the planners as superficial approaches which, at best, cured only symptoms and not basic causes.

His view was that the Depression had been brought about by the devotion of the people to materialistic goals; the real solution to the economic crisis then was to abandon the false gods of money and property and focus attention on the development of "inner resources," to place value not on possessions but on self-dependence, a benevolent interest in the welfare of others, education of the mind, the imagination, and the spirit—returning, in other words, to the ideals which Poole believed had characterized earlier generations of Americans. Really perceptive Americans, he felt, were welcoming the rigors of the Depression because, by taking away their material goods, it was forcing them to rely on their spiritual assets and to discover a new set of values that would bring them real happiness and fulfillment. It is clear that by 1933 he had abandoned his earlier belief in the efficacy of systems of reforming society as a whole and had, in effect, accepted Emerson's belief that progress is essentially a matter of the individual's growth.

Poole decided to dramatize his theory about the evils of material prosperity and spiritual poverty by telling of the breakup of a modern American marriage—one corrupted by materialism—under the stresses of the world-wide economic collapse. As a general source he used the situation currently facing the upper middle class—one which he knew quite well; perhaps he even had a specific family in mind. When he decided to describe life in New England from 1880 to 1900 as a contrast to his picture of life in the subsequent decades, he drew upon memories of his childhood and upon material collected while making his home in New Hampshire. John, the narrator, employs some of Poole's own experiences when he recounts his life story; and many of his anecdotes are to be found elsewhere in the novelist's works: usually true stories, they came from the author's reservoir of tales he himself liked to tell.[3] John Blake, the author's spokes-man, narrates the story of his brother Gilbert's family. To emphasize the changes which have taken place since 1914, he first describes the childhood of the Blakes in the old-fashioned, independent, self-sufficient New England of the pre-World War I era. Then he returns to the present, and the rest of the book becomes the story of the demoralization of Gil in the sum-mer of 1932.

Gilbert had been a prominent creative architect, but he had become materialistic in response to the demands of a free-spend-ing era and a greedy family. After the death in 1921 of Myra—the mother of his three children, Ruth, Ned, and Elliott—he had married Natalie Ames, a very attractive and expensive widow. But after ten years of marriage Gil finds himself at fifty-five with most of his assets frozen in unsalable real estate. The building boom is over; people no longer have need of an architect. But his family is as demanding as ever. To complicate the situation, Natalie is gradually shifting her affections to Paul Fowler, who has made a fortune by selling short on the crashing market. Gil desperately tries to support his wife in her accustomed style, thus sinking further into debt.

He is on the point of having a nervous breakdown when his daughter Ruth arrives from Ohio demanding a large loan to keep her husband, Harold, from going bankrupt and losing his manu-facturing firm. As Ruth and Natalie struggle to gain control of Gil and his money, they evince no consideration for his mental condition. At last Ruth wins; Gil sells his lovely house and finances Harold's company. Natalie calmly departs for Europe (and Fowler), certain that no crisis can ever make such changes that an attractive woman will be unable to find a man to give her more than her share.

The loss of his wife leaves Gil bitter and without faith in any-thing. John's consolation that human troubles are of small im-portance when seen in the perspective of history or of eternity gives him little satisfaction. Under his brother's guidance, how-ever, Gil gains a new interest in life: his son Ned is educating the boys at his preparatory school to be open-minded and cap-able of adapting themselves to whatever changes may come in the uncertain world of the future. *Great Winds* ends with Gil partly recovered and with new faith in life. The "ghost of property" has been laid.

Great Winds is a failure in nearly every way but particularly as an attempt to dramatize a thesis. First, Poole's basic contention —that the world's troubles are the result of materialism—is true only in a very general sense and completely disregards the many other factors which produced such events as the purging of liberty from Russia, the terrorist activities of the Fascists, and the appearance of breadlines in America. Second, even his argument that the actions of Gil's dependents are the result of this spirit of materialism is not really illustrated by the story; instead, one is left with the conviction that in the case of these people their incredible selfishness—although reinforced by the money-madness of the era and triggered by the failure of the economic system—is a result of flaws within the characters themselves and not just the times in which they live. Third, his attempts to bring into the story the events of the outside world, usually by having John tell of what he has seen abroad, lack immediacy because they are told at second hand and seem like the artificial plot contrivances which they obviously are; furthermore, the effect of these digressions into subjects like Bolshevism, Mussolini, and the League of Nations interrupts the narrative.

Poole's chief mistake in presenting his thesis was, of course, selecting an upper-class family that would escape most of the impact of the Depression. The real tragedy of the 1930's occurred in the homes of the lower and middle classes, and the most dangerous aspect of the period was that there were fifteen million desperate men ready to follow a Hitler or a Lenin. But Poole did not write a *Grapes of Wrath*. Instead, he dealt with a tiny minority of the population and told how hard times forced his characters to sell their extra homes or temporarily cost them most of their income from preferred stock. Why did the man who had made his reputation by pleading the cause of the common worker in *The Harbor* barely mention him in this book? Perhaps he felt, as Howells had felt almost twenty years before, that he was too old to write an honest book about the proletariat. More to the point, Poole may have believed that he could not tell their story because he had no firsthand knowledge of the lives, desires, and needs of urban laborers or migrant workers or poor farmers of the West. The explanation was certainly not indifference: one needs only to recall his hearty activities in the cause of the Frontier Nursing Service, his campaigns for the Bowery YMCA and Salvation Army, and his eye-witness descriptions of breadlines in letters to the *New York Times* to dispel any notions that he considered himself above the mob or was unconcerned with its hunger. But, whatever his reasons may have been, he missed a chance to write a significant book about the 1930's.

When evaluated solely as a piece of fiction, *Great Winds* is equally disappointing and unsatisfying, mostly because of its unrelieved dreariness. The early pages, which are filled with realistic details of life in rural New England, are the best in the book and move rapidly, but the rest of the novel impresses the reader as unduly long and too slow moving because the plot is too slight for the space it occupies. The ugliness of the motives of the two women and the strain on the mentally exhausted Gil are well handled and are remembered long after the book is read, but too many pages are devoted to their tormenting of the victim. And since the sordid outcome is obvious from the first, the reader soon shares Gil's hopelessness and sense of futility. This mood is so firmly established that the mild, abstract philosophizing of John cannot convince the reader that Gil, freed of the bonds of earthly goods, will undergo a spiritual rebirth and be a better man in the end.

Poole might have been spared complete failure if he had been able to make his "good" characters strong enough to defeat the "bad" ones. But, as in the case of *The Hunter's Moon,* he was able to make the villains depressingly real but unable to give the proponents of his ideals a fighting chance. The nagging relentless Ruth, driven by the blind determination to protect her offspring, is an outstanding portrait; the wife, although almost a type character, is nevertheless wholly believable. By contrast, Gil is a weakling; and John is never more than a shadowy observer, a bloodless reincarnation of Grandfather Wade. It is understandable then why Gil's recovery under John's guidance is not convincing.

Of the reviews of *Great Winds* at least half were unfavorable. The consensus was that Poole had not written a novel but a tract on the problem of the times. In so doing, he sadly neglected both his story and his characters. At least one reviewer found

Poole's views to be conventional, naïve, and shallow—and not much consolation to the suffering. In general, the reviews were not so harsh as, with justice, they might have been. The readers did not share the benevolence of the critics, however, and they bought only about four thousand copies of *Great Winds.*

III One of Us

On September 4, 1934, sixteen months after *Great Winds* was published, Poole produced a second novel about the Depression, *One of Us,* a work of surprising solidity and workmanship which almost achieves a place with his best work. Part of this success may be attributed to his familiarity with its material. He had been visiting in New Hampshire since 1907 and spending summers near Franconia since 1911; in that time he had collected many anecdotes and observed many character types. Some of these he used without great success in *Great Winds* and in magazine stories. Finally, he hit upon the idea of telling the story of the area from the point of view of a native storekeeper— a man who would know practically everything that had happened in the community. The choice of this central character was not accidental, for among the writer's friends were Wilbur Parker and his son, Ned, the proprietors of the Franconia General Store. Thus the Parkers became models for the fictional Willoughby Gale and his son, Ted Gale. Ned Parker's wife, who was responsible for the modernizing of the old country store, supplied part of the character of Leila Gale, the wife of Ted Gale.[4] Another character in *One of Us,* John Valliant, a Free Baptist clergyman, is one of Poole's friends—Samuel Nickerson. In short, a substantial number of the events and people are drawn, with a few changes, from life, as a glance at *The Bridge* or *The Great White Hills* will show. Undoubtedly, more prolonged study would disclose sources for many more items in the novel.

Poole was careful to keep his locale authentic. He used the Parker's store as a setting and reproduced it in detail. While he was making notes, he was permitted to look over the credit books; from them he was able to collect details about a time in New England (1880-1910) that he did not know personally.[5] Yet in spite of the fact that he did much research and often copied real life onto his pages, even the careful reader would never notice the fact, for he assimilated his materials skillfully.

In *One of Us*, Ted Gale grows up in the unmechanized, unhurried, unregimented rural New Hampshire of the 1880's; marries his childhood sweetheart, Leila; and assumes the role of community leader. But for Leila the call of the world is too strong, and after ten years she leaves Ted and her two children to become a "muckraker" and then a correspondent covering the Japanese war in 1905 and the world events which followed. Leila returns only for visits; the world of change has struck its first blow at the hero.

But life goes on for Ted; as time passes, the author mentions in an unobtrusive manner many of the historical events which are about to remake the world. Even in the hills the modern world intrudes with new roads, automobiles, milk inspection, and improved education. Ted, Junior, is developing into a man with a brilliant future as a scientific farmer. But the technical and industrial developments which make life better for millions also lead to struggles over markets and raw materials, the conflicts that help to produce World War I. When his son dies in France, the father is almost broken by grief. But with the grim determination that is his chief trait, he returns to his daily work and after many years finds solace in the children of his daughter, Ann. Leila, however, is permanently embittered by young Ted's useless sacrifice. She has seen the peace lost at Versailles. Out of the great idealism of the Wilson era has come only the pompous materialism of the 1920's.

To Ted the period is one in which he must resist the power of chain stores and the temptation to acquire easy money. In spite of his wife's warning that the vast system of credit and airy speculation will bring disaster, Ted, like so many others, speculates in real estate—and is caught in 1929. In this situation he finds that he has the inner resources which make possible a very simple life. Like Roger Gale in *His Family*, he finds himself possessing youthful vigor when he must support singlehandedly the members of his daughter's family, who have lived so long on Easy Street that they have no inner strength or capacity for self-dependence. Led by Franklin D. Roosevelt in the White House, a sadder and wiser Ted Gale and others like him begin the long climb out of the Depression. The outside world has taken his wife, his son, half his life, and his business sense; but he has learned that a firm adherence to old-fashioned ideals and the pursuit of a simple life unburdened with useless possessions will enable him to face the future.

One of Us strikes the delicate balance which Poole sought between pure fiction and dramatized ideas. The book has a didactic purpose: the story is supposed to demonstrate how one man has withstood the forces of change originally described in *The Harbor*. The reader of *One of Us* is supposed to learn a lesson from this story: those who "ride out the storm" will do so only if they reject materialism and develop a capacity for endurance, hard work, faith, and spiritual depth. In other words, this novel is a statement and demonstration of the same ideas advanced in *Great Winds.*

But *One of Us* is much more convincing in its ideology and certainly less painful to absorb than its predecessor because the author allows the life story of the central character to put across the theme without authorial interference. John Blake in the earlier novel was not a believable person, not the narrator of a good story, nor an exemplification of the ideas he wished to convey. Ted Gale is all of these, and therein lies the reason for the success of *One of Us*. Poole never editorializes but lets Gale tell his own story; the hero's personality soon emerges clearly as he recounts his childhood ideals, his hopes, his failures, his reactions to these experiences, and his eventual discovery of the path he and all men must follow in the existing predicament.

The storekeeper has his faults—excessive conservatism, stubbornness, a quick temper; but he is also reliable, honest, and strong. He speaks in the words, nasal accent, and rhythm of the New Englander; his homely philosophy is constantly entertaining and yet impressive; his grim understatement of his grief when his son dies is more painful than pages of rant. Most important, he is not Ernest Poole in disguise, as are some of the author's spokesmen. He is a fully independent personality with experiences and ideas unlike his creator's. If his conclusions concerning life and the problems of change are like those of the novelist, it is because the events of his lifetime have led him to think in a similar manner.

In another way Gale is unlike most of Poole's characters: he does not alter his outlook as, for example, Billy does in *The*

Harbor. As a young man Ted is cautious, independent, slow in making up his mind. A Democrat, he works for better roads and schools but opposes federal intervention in local affairs. During the 1920's he is wary of the loose credit practices used by chain stores to take away his trade; he will always help those who need it, but he dreads debt. As he puts the idea, "I want to say it's a lonesome game being independent in such times." Even his cautious land investments are motivated by the belief that land is safer than stocks and by the conviction that a land boom will result in jobs for the people of the community. After 1929 he is the only one in his family with experience in cutting expenses drastically; but he is also the only local businessman who extends credit to his customers when they really need it: "Life grew tough and hard, but our dander was up and we wouldn't give in." Even his acceptance of Roosevelt is cautious, for he knows that only the people can save themselves. Thus he remains consistent—a completely believable character whom Poole created without ever entering the story as author or commentator.

One of Us has, however, several crucial weaknesses which prevent its complete success. One is the fact that only one person is consistently vivid and well-rounded—the narrator. The minor characters suffer a loss of reality because they are seen solely from Gale's point of view and are brought in only when the story demands that they influence the central figure. As a result, such characters as his crippled father and old Valliant are distinct and animated when first introduced but gradually lose any lifelike qualities and become mere names. His daughter Ann, by contrast, is given little attention when she is a child and becomes real to the reader only after she becomes a married woman and a burden for her father in the Depression.

A second weakness—though a minor one—is that the book attempts to cover too many events and too long a period—almost sixty years. The story is held together, however, by the central figure and by the considerable emphasis laid on the three main events which alter the narrator's life. In general, the reader today does not feel that he is being hurried along as he does when he reads *Blind.* When he has finished the book, he feels that he has read a competent and complete account of the evolution of life in New England since 1880.

A third weakness is an absence of plot; in other words, there is only a series of events without a definite climax or turning point. Poole chose this form of artless narrative deliberately, for he intended the book to be simply the everyday story of an average life: only in art (the reader might add, "and in retrospect") are there crucial moments of high drama and decisions on which the entire course of events turns. One result of the deliberate avoidance of plot, the writer's strongest device, was a lessening of dramatic impact. The story loses its hold after the death of Ted's son, partly because the reader realizes that, having survived that shock, Gale is not likely to be broken by subsequent events; in other words, the suspense is gone. Yet in spite of the absence of an artificial plot (or perhaps because of it) *One of Us* is often deeply moving in its sincerity and truthfulness. A sense of humor, a freedom from undigested or irrelevant authorial comments, the reality of the main character, and the competent, artless narrative flow make up for the fact that Poole chose to forget a conventional plot.

One of Us received an unusually large number of reviews, indicating perhaps that the novel was considered a successful "comeback." Not since *The Harbor*, said one critic, had Poole written a novel so compelling and penetrating. While it lacked the magic of the former book, said another, *One of Us* was a likable, strong, quiet novel. The conservative *Booklist* recommended it for hospital reading because it was so calm, human, and encouraging in outlook. And most of the reviewers agreed that "pleasant" and "satisfying" were the correct adjectives to describe it.

But for others the story was entirely too peaceful. They protested that the novelist belonged to the sugar-sweet New England school of Harold B. Wright and Clarence B. Kelland, and hoped to hold his audience by looking at the world with a hazy optimism and by exhorting people to return to the "simple life" and the "old ideals." The "stern New Englander seeing it through" belonged in romantic fiction, not in a realistic picture of modern life. The reader was advised to examine the work of William Faulkner as an antidote to New England fudge. In spite of the fact that several critics lavished praise on the style and characterization and predicted a large sale, the total did not reach four thousand copies. The time was not a good one for novels— especially those written by Ernest Poole.

IV The Bridge

A bigger disappointment followed: sixteen months later, on January 4, 1936, a new work, a novelette entitled *The House That Grew Young*, was refused by the Macmillan Company. According to George P. Britt, the president of the company and a personal friend of the author, none of the twelve readers on the staff could find any basis for its publication. Britt urged his friend to write another book like *The Harbor* and declared his confidence in his ability to do so, provided that he gave himself enough time.[6] Poole replied that he did not think that the story was poor, that he was not ashamed of it even though it was not a work of major importance, and that it had a better chance of selling than *One of Us*. Apparently he was considerably discouraged by the setback, for he declared that any future work was in "the lap of the Gods."[7] The novel was subsequently offered to Houghton Mifflin and refused. The manuscript was apparently then destroyed, and today even the Poole family cannot recall what its subject was.

During the remainder of 1936 Poole turned, with fair success, to the composition of short stories for various magazines; then, in February, 1937, he announced plans for a new novel.[8] Seemingly, little or nothing was done on it; instead, he went abroad as a correspondent in the summer; and, indeed, for the next twelve years he did no work on any long pieces of fiction. It is clear that by this time his writing was showing the effect of his growing conviction that he had lost his ability as a novelist; according to William Poole, perhaps equally important was the fact that he spent much of his time studying stock market reports and planning cautious new investments in an effort to recoup his losses. By the time of his death in 1950 he had, to nearly everyone's surprise, largely succeeded; but his writing had suffered in the process.

In the spring of 1938[9] he began work on his memoirs, *The Bridge: My Own Story*, which appeared on August 13, 1940—his first published book since 1934. His return to writing was clearly motivated by more important considerations than a desire to tell his life story, for the emphasis in *The Bridge* is placed on world events rather than on his own experiences. During his trips abroad as a magazine correspondent in the late 1930's, he had visited

Mussolini's Italy for the second time and France during a period of toppling governments and economic paralysis brought on by the omnipotence of labor unions. What he had seen convinced him that war between the dictators and the democracies was inevitable; accordingly, when he returned, he began work on one more book—his autobiography—to alert the free world (as he had done so often) to its peril and to reaffirm his belief in the "inner resources" of free men—courage, intelligence, the willingness to die for a dream. Thus *The Bridge* reflects the spirit of the author at the end of the 1930's—tired, discouraged, but never completely unsure that men, if they know the truth, will act in a way admirable beyond all expectations. He decided to use his own life story and the events he had witnessed in order to illustrate his thesis that the twentieth century, shaped by new and barely understood forces, was a time of continuing tense situations, each of which must be met with courage, resignation to change, and faith that out of the upheavals would come a better world. He described the sixty years of his life as a temporal bridge between the settled and peaceful past and the tumultuous, uncertain future; he closed with a stirring admonition to young men to press bravely on across the bridge into the new age with readiness for any crisis. The resemblance between the autobiography and *The Harbor*, with its challenge to Americans to sail out into unknown seas, is obvious.

The Bridge is a book with many flaws, the least of which is its journalistic style. A more serious matter is that one learns too little about the novelist's personality, certainly a surprising weakness in an autobiography but one to be expected in a book more concerned with observations than with the observer. Even a cursory examination shows a disproportionate number of pages devoted to the years from 1900 to 1920, while the important years in which he did most of his writing are relegated to eighty-six pages of rambling anecdotes which convey little or no information about his career as a novelist. One explanation might be that Poole considered the years beginning with his work in the tenements and covering the Russian Revolutions, the writing of *The Harbor*, and World War I the most significant period. Possibly, too, he felt in 1940 that he had failed as a novelist and wished to emphasize his years of fame. In any case, the structure and content of *The Bridge* were also dictated by his decision to save work by borrowing heavily from material he had already composed and published in magazines and books; for this reason the autobiography is crowded with details in chapters dealing with certain phases of his life and uninformative in others when his memory and energy failed. Thus, a person who had read the articles on tuberculosis in New York slums, the Russian Revolution, and World War I, or the semi-autobiographical novels finds much of *The Bridge* dull and repetitious.

Furthermore, the dates of events are often not given, and information important to a biographer is missing or inaccurate. To the literary researcher *The Bridge* is, of course, disappointing. Of the twenty books published before 1940 only six (*The Harbor, His Family, Blind, The Avalanche, Silent Storms, Nurses on Horseback*) are mentioned by name or discussed at any length. By inference or close reading one may uncover data on the composition and origins of *His Second Wife,* "*The Dark People,*" *The Village, Beggars' Gold, Danger, The Little Dark Man, The Destroyer, Great Winds, One of Us,* and *The Great White Hills of New Hampshire* and some of the short stories and articles. But of several of the best novels little or nothing can be discovered.

Yet the scholar is thankful for these hints. They enable him to study the extent to which the writer used real people and events in his works. There are, moreover, recollections of Woodrow Wilson, O. Henry, Mark Twain, Maxim Gorky, Big Bill Haywood, Robert Frost, William Dean Howells, Ray Stannard Baker, and Lincoln Steffens—to mention only a few. And the reader who has no previous acquaintance with Poole finds the anecdotal method and the materials well worth perusal, particularly since the style is clear and direct.

The critical notices of *The Bridge* were usually polite summaries of the author's life which pointed out that *The Harbor* had been a best-seller a quarter of a century earlier and that Poole had won a Pulitzer Prize for *His Family:* they appeared to be more a tribute to a veteran writer than a response to an important book. Several critics praised *The Bridge* as a very readable collection of human interest stories about people, both the famous and the unknown; others liked the capable way in which he had sketched in his characters and scenes. But the book seemed otherwise unimportant and offered little in the way of a plan for defending the free world. Several young liberals made fun of Poole's pre-1920 idealism: rhetorical affirmations were less than useless, they said; only practical social doctrines could save the world.

It must have been a shock to Poole when he read that he had led a "full and useful life of romantic groping" in which he never came to terms with the facts of life or even mastered reporting. As if to drive home the point that his life was a failure and his name forgotten, only slightly over two thousand copies of *The Bridge* were purchased—many of them by libraries; autobiographies of minor figures rarely sell better, but Poole felt that Macmillan's had in recent years made little effort to sell his works. It was no wonder that, in the hope of better promotion of his books, he soon after turned to a new publisher. This decision, made in a time of real discouragement, opened for Ernest Poole a whole new career.[10]

CHAPTER 9

Life Resurgent: The Last Decade

O N JANUARY 23, 1940, Poole celebrated his sixtieth birthday and began the last decade of his life. It was a period filled with tragedy for the world, the nation, and the writer's family, especially when his son-in-law was killed early in World War II. One would imagine that these disasters, coupled with the disappointments of the preceding era, would have made these last years gloomy and embittered; but, in fact, Poole during the war years experienced a rejuvenation and a love for life that impressed his family and acquaintances and that continues to astound the readers of his three books and many short pieces written at this time. The war itself—a new crusade for freedom—seems to have been the major influence in his renewed interest in life.

After the loss of the peace at Versailles, the subsequent disillusionment of the 1920's, and the decline of democracies and simultaneous rise of dictatorships in the 1930's, Poole had lost heart; but freedom-loving peoples at last proved what he had always believed—that, in spite of its weaknesses and inefficiencies, government of the people would prevail. Filled with an enthusiasm that had been dormant since the days of America's entry into the first war, Poole obtained a commission from *Redbook* and from the North American Newspaper Alliance to visit England in 1940 during the German air attacks and again in 1941; his agents list ten articles and stories which resulted; but, for some reason, only a few ever saw print. Back home, he continued to write pieces concerned with the war and even tried, but without success, to secure a position under Elmer Davis in the Office of War Information. Stimulated by getting "out of the workroom and back into life," he began to look for a new literary form and material that would interest him. By chance he found both without difficulty and spent his last happy years in assembling non-fictional works about two of his favorite subjects: Chicago in the legendary past and New Hampshire, past and present.

I Giants Gone

The first of these books, *Giants Gone: The Men Who Made Chicago,* published on February 15, 1943, was the brainchild of Poole's son, William Morris Poole, who was at that time editor-in-chief at Whittlesey House. William pointed out to his father that his recollections of Chicago and his many contacts there made him particularly qualified to write a book about the city and its famous people. Poole accepted the commission, and together they worked on the organization. Their first problem—to select about twenty personages for inclusion—proved to be somewhat complicated because Poole decided that *Giants Gone* should be a continuous narrative about the growth of Chicago rather than a series of unconnected biographies.

He planned to place his "giants" in chronological order and insert in the sketch of each person the significant events which happened during his lifetime. The result, he hoped, would be an interweaving of history and biography which would show the important men as the products and the molders of their times. The problems presented by his approach were many. The first was to find people of importance to represent each stage of the city's development—and sometimes this meant resurrecting rather obscure men. Equally difficult was the selection of figures in special areas of endeavor—art, music, medicine, crime, reform, or social work. Moreover, there was the necessity of finding colorful characters whose exploits would make lively reading. In spite of the difficulty of the task the Pooles eventually selected twenty Chicagoans for the study.

After the planning stage, Poole began research. As his list of sources indicates, he drew material from a large number of books. He also spent months interviewing relatives, descendants, and acquaintances of his subjects, a task he enjoyed and at which he was particularly skilled. Many of the "old timers" recalled clearly the years following the Civil War, and he gained much graphic detail from them. He was also able to draw upon the legacy of anecdotes which his father, a matchless storyteller, had told to him in earlier years.

After he had collected (in his usual fashion) a great pile of note cards, he began the writing of *Giants Gone*. Composing a good biography is not easy, especially when one's space is limited to about a dozen pages. His procedure was to decide upon the picture he wished to give of each man and then to select such anecdotes and incidents as would convey that image most effectively. When his character sketches were completed, he began to weave in the historical background. Finally, when he was satisfied with organization and content, he began to polish and rewrite until the style was free of awkwardness.

Giants Gone is not an awe-inspiring work; it is merely a readable, entertaining book. The organization does not distract but instead contributes to the effectiveness of the presentation. Each personality is adequately and thoughtfully described and illustrated; the historical events are narrated with sureness and ease. Finally, because of the care lavished on the style, *Giants Gone* leaves an impression of workmanship which is missing from an earlier attempt at nonfiction, "Captain Dollar." In short, it is a book which the author could be proud of.

Giants Gone received a fair number of reviews, most of which were enthusiastic. The *New York Herald Tribune* gave it a front page spread in its book review section, an honor few of his works were ever awarded. His character drawings were called "the best collection of biographical sketches ever done about Chicagoans," and he was complimented for bringing the people to life, for showing them as human beings rather than as "disembodied economic forces."

One reviewer, however, suggested that the author had concealed the actual boom-town crudity of Chicago behind a veil of nostalgic charm. Another critic, obviously a purist, evinced a distaste for books "which straddle the line between objective history and popular narrative." He affirmed that *Giants Gone* was not "integrated in terms of any significant perspective" and therefore added little to an understanding of the builders of Chicago. Many reviewers, however, recognized that the book was not intended to be a precise and scholarly evaluation of facts but, rather, a series of living portraits. Thus there was praise for the work and enthusiasm over the more flamboyant figures of the early days, men whose stories read like folklore.

The *Library Journal* predicted accurately that the book would be of interest to many types of readers. In all, about eighty-five hundred copies were sold, and two of the biographies were later reprinted in anthologies.[2] The book was well received in Chicago, where it had larger advance sales than he had hoped; his fear that it would be less successful nationally proved groundless.[3]

II The Great White Hills

In the early years of World War II, Howard Cady, an editor at Doubleday and Company, began work on a project dear to his heart—a series of books about mountain areas. After he had commissioned the volume on Vermont, he approached William Poole and asked him to see whether his father, whose thoroughness, capability, and reliability had impressed him, was interested in adding New Hampshire to the series. Poole soon began the task, which was to occupy most of four years.[4]

William Poole has said that Cady had been anxious to obtain his father's services because he had "the right flavor." In other words, he felt that Poole would be able to achieve the goal of the local colorist: to convey to the reader the peculiar characteristics of a people and a region. This was an accurate estimate because the author had already demonstrated his knowledge of New England in a handful of magazine pieces and in the very competent novel, *One of Us*. This knowledge had been garnered in the more than thirty years since the building of his summer cottage near Franconia. From lawyers, doctors, storekeepers, and old residents, indeed from all the local inhabitants who had gradually accepted him as a friend and neighbor, he had accumulated both stories and insights into these people and their lives. Poole's son has said that his father had not thought of doing a book on New Hampshire until he was asked to do so by Cady, but he must have welcomed the opportunity to use his backlog of material and to commemorate his adopted homeland.[5]

Howard Cady was not interested in a guidebook of the sort the Federal Writers Project had produced. Instead, he wanted a work which combined folklore, history, descriptions, and the atmosphere of the locale. Such an assignment meant that Poole could employ "human interest" material extensively, but it also presented a serious problem in organization. To prevent *The Great White Hills* from becoming a hodgepodge of anecdotes, Poole divided his subject into seventeen subdivisions, a plan which served to facilitate the collecting of data and to give form to the finished product.

Poole's research required several years, but his composition took even more time and was the most tiresome process of all. The notes had to be absorbed into a series of smoothly written essays that would capture and hold the interest of the reader. The final product appeared on May 23, 1946. After an introductory chapter, which describes some of his early experiences in New Hampshire, are accounts of the early days of exploration, settlement, and Indian warfare. These are followed by chapters on the lumber barons' pillage of the forests and the successful efforts of the conservationists. Having covered the chief historical matters, Poole then turns to a delineation of New England character in sections labeled "Battling Sins," "Crimes and Quarrels," "Doctoring," and "Mountain Politics." Other sections describe the barren lives on hill farms and in mountain towns. There are also divisions dealing with winter sports, wild life, mountain climbing, weather observatories, mountain stores, the school system (as always, one of his favorite topics), and the development of transportation over the years. In short, almost every imaginable aspect of New Hampshire finds a place in the book.

Otto Mallery said that *The Great White Hills of New Hampshire* is the standard work on the subject and one that will not soon be surpassed. The average reader will find Poole's book entertaining and informative and will find much to fascinate him in the narrative sections. Long a master of the orally delivered anecdote, Poole showed in the many vignettes included in this book that he was equally skilled in the writing of short tales. Ranging from comedy and bawdy humor to the darkest tragedy, and told with stark realism and the startling economy of a ballad, these pieces pierce deeply into human suffering and decay or expound with Dickensian delight upon the joys of good food and drink or upon the extent of human folly.

Unforgettable is the array of characters whose deeds and words have been preserved in oral tradition. One legendary figure was Old Colorado, a prostitute who "serviced" forty lumbermen in one evening. Another, lost in antiquity, was the disgusted farmer who vehemently proclaimed, "God damn the son of a bitch who took these hills from the Indians." Then there was a man so determined to commit suicide that he climbed out on a tree limb, placed a noose around his neck as an extra precaution, and then shot himself in the head. In another chilling scene a man who has pinched pennies all his life learns that he is dying of cancer and resolves on suicide to avoid further suffering. But, when he discovers that five rifle shells will cost ten cents, he almost gives up his plan. Finally, however, after weighing his fear of pain against his dread of spending money, he grimly declares, "They're wuth it." These vignettes are probably the most fascinating sketches the author ever wrote.

A second reason for the success of the book is that the pictures of New Hampshire are seen through the eyes of the author or, at least, colored and enlivened by his attitudes and personality. Almost every page reflects a vigor, strength, and robust good humor one would not expect to find in a man in his middle sixties. He demonstrates an infectious enthusiasm for life, a confidence and self-assurance that warmed the hearts of all who admired him. In this book there is no decline into bitterness and death, no fading away of a tired old writer. *The Great White Hills* is as fresh and youthful as anything he ever wrote. There is none of the inadequacy and weariness one feels in *The Bridge*, a work written barely six years before.

The Poole one sees in this book is a man who has gained the maturity so many of his characters sought. He still holds the same Emersonian conceptions of man's relation to men and to the universe, but the statement of his views now carries conviction. There is little of the "ivory tower" in his attitudes: he has acquired a Rabelaisian taste for the bawdy that might have improved his novels if it had appeared sooner; he does not hesitate to write with photographic realism of the ugliness of the world, and he does not turn his eyes away from unpleasantness as he seemed to do earlier in life. One might describe him as a "hardened optimist" who, after years of observing man's deeds, has weighed his depravity against his achievements and found him more good than bad. As a philosopher, he is tolerant of small sins, chary of judging his fellow men, a believer in the God in the hearts of men of good will. Poole had seen two world wars and an enervating economic depression; but he had also seen a few men, here and there, win out in spite of losses, death, and countless personal tragedies. He has no illusions about mankind, only an undying hope for the race.

The reviewers gave a favorable reaction to *The Great White Hills of New Hampshire,* largely on the basis of its anecdotes and vignettes, a fact which inspired some to remark that books about people were always preferable to those about terrain. The quality of the prose—described as "distinguished" and "poetic"—did not escape attention. In fact, some of the critics found Poole's enthusiastic treatment of New Hampshire so infectious that they predicted many readers would go to the state either as tourists or as settlers. This reception by the critics was equaled by that of the public, who purchased approximately twenty thousand copies, put the book on the best-seller list of 1946, and made it one of the author's most popular works.

III   The Nancy Flyer

Poole's last published work, *The Nancy Flyer: A Stagecoach Epic* (copyrighted January 27, 1949), grew out of a suggestion by his son that he write about the heyday of the stagecoach in the New England area. Countless books, stories, and motion pictures had made this vehicle a fixture in the romance of the West; but few people were aware that in Europe and in America, for at least one hundred years, regularly scheduled coaches had been the only form of public transportation and that one of the most colorful and famous lines in the world had, during the 1830's, run the famed Concord coaches from the coast up into the White Mountain vacation area.

Poole accepted the commission, not because he wanted to enlighten the American public but because he had already in his possession a great deal of material about the subject—information left over from the preceding book. He had heard tales of the daredevil drivers and their escapades; he had seen, still standing, the very inns at which travelers had stopped to change horses and refresh themselves; he had even carefully examined a beautiful old coach now relegated to a barn and thus had ready a model for the "Nancy Flyer"; and he also knew where he could find in books whatever additional material he needed.[6]

When the research was completed, he had at his fingertips many of the details needed for a social history of New Hampshire from 1830 to 1870. He was ready with material describing the food, alcoholic beverages, costumes, popular songs; techniques for breeding, breaking, and driving horses; manufacture, cost, and appearance of mail coaches; the political issues of the day; the character of the stage drivers; and even the morals of actresses. His problem was, of course, that the public would in all probability not be interested in an extended sociological essay; obviously, a solution was to invent a plot and characters and use the material as the background of a novel.

The plot, according to the introduction, is concerned with "a lifelong battle between a man and a woman, a coach and an inn, a home and the road." Narrated by Sam Hubbard, the son of the heroine, the story covers the period from 1835 to 1880 and tells of Nancy Hubbard, a lusty widow who runs the Bull Moose Inn, and her relationship with Bob Gale, a colorful but footloose coach driver. Nancy is determined to make a success of her inn and find a second husband who will fill her house with children. In time Bob succumbs to her obvious attributes—a prosperous inn and an attractive form—and then persuades her to finance the purchase of the most beautiful stage coach ever manufactured by the Concord firm, Abbot and Downing. Named the "Nancy Flyer," the coach is instrumental in blighting Nancy's hopes: a ride over a rough road causes a miscarriage which leaves her barren, and Bob's obsession with his coach so occupies his mind that the business suffers and the couple are soon in debt. By the 1850's the first railroad has pushed into the valley and made the "Nancy Flyer" obsolete, thus ending an exciting era. The remainder of the book takes Bob and his stepson through the Civil War and then to the West during the golden days of the stagecoach in that area. The story ends with the arrival of Bob's archenemy, the railroad, this time the Union Pacific.

The Nancy Flyer is assuredly not one of Poole's better works. In fact, it can hardly be considered a novel; it is a well documented social history in which a very slight story is lost in the detailed and lengthy background. The plot—supposedly a "lifelong conflict"—is seen in operation only in the early pages; after the initial confrontation of Nancy and the "Flyer," Poole seems to have forgotten what he set out to do. The time scheme has a grave weakness in that it is much too extended; the pace is so rapid that the few potentially dramatic scenes are presented as mere anecdotes; the sequence of events does not even arrive at a climax. The main personages never come to life for more than a moment, and the narrator constantly drops out of character, especially when discussing his mother's sex life. Several themes with dramatic possibilities make an appearance, capture the reader's attention, and then are discarded. As a result, one is not sure whether the main theme is the "lifelong conflict," the tragedy of a barren woman, the growth to maturity of a stepson in a divided family, or the evil effects of the machine age on the age of romance. Even the style is awkward, in many places a hasty rewriting of notes—a weakness particularly evident in the long, tiresome descriptive passages.

The critics treated *The Nancy Flyer* very gently and limited themselves to short summaries and to such comments as "an innocent and nostalgic little story" and "as gay as an old-fashioned valentine or a Currier and Ives print." The *Booklist* put it on a roster of books for children, apparently without squeamishness over the rather crude and vulgar treatment of sex. Other reviewers commented that the story had "heroic dimensions" and "epic quality" and suggested that it was worth reading. Many of the reviewers, however, pointed out that there was an overabundance of background material and history and not enough about the characters and their adventures; but they added that they found the factual material so fascinating that they could overlook the weak plot. While not a work that would add to the author's laurels, it was one that would interest those who liked lively tales and those attracted to accounts of the romantic past in New England. As a matter of fact, *The Nancy Flyer* proved to be rather popular and sold about nine thousand copies. Many flaws in the book can be attributed to the state of the author's health during its composition. Poole had, since 1945, been suffering from high blood pressure and was bothered by insomnia; then in 1949 he suffered a slight stroke. Urged on by the fear that he might not live to complete his story of the stagecoach and another novel he had planned, he wrote rapidly. This overwork contributed to his last stroke, which came in the autumn of 1948, four days after he had completed his revisions of *The Nancy Flyer*. For over a year he was in a state approaching mental incompetence, his body gradually succumbing to paralysis. His twenty-fifth book, a story of a country doctor and his experiences with the unknown forces that reside in men, was never begun. On January 10, 1950, he died at his apartment at 139 East Sixty-sixth Street in New York City, just thirteen days before his seventieth birthday.[9]

CHAPTER *10*

Conclusion

B ECAUSE a novelist's literary reputation among his contem-
poraries may depend on his ability to produce a number of
successful works of fiction, Poole's achievements in "non-fiction"
during the 1940's did not revive his former fame. As a matter of
fact, the obituaries, for the most part, noted only that he had
once been acclaimed as the author of *The Harbor* and the first
Pulitzer Prize novel; the works of the subsequent thirty years
were not even mentioned, and the fact that during that period
he had written several excellent novels was still not recognized.
Although his position today in American literature has not much
improved, the capriciousness of fame and literary reputation will
not always obscure the accomplishments of this man whose name
few now remember. Many of his books and shorter pieces gave
pleasure and entertainment to his readers; some, like *The Harbor*,
helped to shape the thought of his generation and offered insight
into the trends and movements of a confusing era. More important, his better works give that indescribable enjoyment which
comes only from compositions of genuine merit. Nor is the example he set without meaning: he was a man who chose a
career and kept working toward his goal, according to his own
standards, in spite of ostensible failure. Poole displayed a kind of
courage and self-sufficiency which can be admired and emulated.

A number of Poole's works can be recommended without quali-
fication or apology. *With Eastern Eyes* and *The Destroyer* are
superior to many of the American novels now considered
"classics"; and *His Family, Beggars' Gold, Danger,* and *The
Harbor*, though of smaller literary stature, possess the power to
arouse the emotions and to command respect for their solidly constructed pictures of real life, their compellingly accurate charac-

ter portraits, their unsentimental insights into the meaning of human experience. The "non-fiction" works like *The Great White Hills of New Hampshire, The Village,* and *Giants Gone* are informative, accurate, and well-written studies; similarly, the various "novels of ideals"—*The Harbor, Blind, Silent Storms, Great Winds,* and *One of Us*—and the autobiography are invaluable source books for those interested in recent history.

When his fiction is judged by traditional literary standards, much of it is often outstanding. His *forte* was his presentation of women characters, a field in which even literary giants are often notoriously weak; the men, too, were often equally good; and in books like *With Eastern Eyes,* the personalities of even minor characters were drawn with admirable skill. In his choice and presentation of themes—particularly those concerned with the problems of marriage and family relationships—he made memorable contributions. Dialogue, too, even in his earlier novels, but particularly in the later ones, bears witness to his statement that he knew he was writing his best when he could hear the people in a story talking. His style, at first clumsy and corrupted by the low standards of contemporary journalism, eventually attained a simplicity, clarity, and ease which inspire envy in the hearts of those who have tried to write in a similar way. Even in technique Poole on occasion showed mastery. For instance, the limitations of time and space in stories like *Millions,* his experiments with point of view, and, above all, his use of dramatic scenes to advance the plot are the work of a highly skilled professional.

There are serious flaws in some of his works. His fiction can, in certain instances, be justly criticized for such defects as slipshod writing and mishandling of point of view. At times his didacticism is unpleasantly obvious; in some cases it is the ruin of a whole book when he set out to illustrate a thesis about current events and in doing so reduces his characters to puppets, his dialogue to tractarian monologues, and his plots to nothing but sequences of events. Because of these defects, some of his novels deserve to be forgotten; the others do not.

The blame for the lack of recognition of such books as *With Eastern Eyes* and *The Destroyer*—and for the abrupt decline of his reputation—rests with the reviewers, who early accepted the notion that he would never equal his first successes. Blinded by this preconception, they automatically passed judgment beforehand on each new book instead of evaluating it on its own merits. It is true that Poole should never have published a book like *His Second Wife,* but it was grossly unfair of the critics to cite one "potboiler" as proof that the author of *The Harbor* and *His Family* was a hack writer without artistic integrity. Nevertheless, such a book provided ammunition for the reviewers who opposed the author's political and social views and were ready to attack all of his books simply because he had written them.

Others, more interested in current literary fads than in permanent artistic values, rejected his "genteel realism" during the 1920's because the sensational materials and philosophy of the naturalists were in vogue; and during the 1930's his pre-war idealistic socialism seemed hopelessly outdated in the era of the Marxist proletarian novel. Even Poole's supporters were hindered by prejudices, for some would accept nothing except another book like *The Harbor,* while others wanted him to abandon thesis novels and give further pictures of American life like those in *His Family.* In the end no one could evaluate his books objectively; no matter how well he wrote, he was described as "written out." It was inevitable that he would soon be forgotten, particularly when there appeared such consequential novelists as Sinclair Lewis, F. Scott Fitzgerald, Willa Cather, Ernest Hemingway, and—after winning his own fight with the critics—William Faulkner.

The judgment of the literary arbiters—unquestioned until now —was that Poole was not a real star: to them he was just a meteor, burnt out in a brief glory following the publication of *The Harbor.* It seems most unlikely that this view of his literary accomplishments will prevail. In time, more attention will be paid to his better works by scholars and laymen who are capable of objective evaluations, gifted with perspective, and unmoved by the ephemeral fads of the early years of this century. Then, I believe, Poole will be reinstated in the literature books, and the history of the decline of his reputation will be cited as a warning against hasty and ill-formed judgments.

Notes and References

Chapter One

1. Unless otherwise noted, the sources of the biographical information in this volume are Ernest Poole's autobiography, *The Bridge* (New York, 1940), and interviews with his wife, Margaret Ann; his son, William Morris; his close friend, O. T. Mallery; and his sister, Mrs. Bertha Weyl. This last interview was reported to me by Briscoe R. Smith.

2. Charles C. Baldwin, *The Men Who Make Our Novels* (New York, 1919), pp. 27-32.

3. "An Author's Predicament," *Nassau Literary Magazine* (December, 1899), pp. 275-81.

4. Letter to Josephine K. Piercy published in her book, *Modern Writers at Work* (New York, 1930), pp. 535-36.

5. Ray S. Baker, *Woodrow Wilson* (New York, 1927), pp. 9-10, 12.

Chapter Two

1. The pamphlet is *Child Labor: The Street* (New York, 1903). The articles are "Waifs of the Street," *McClure's Magazine*, XXI (May, 1903), 40-48; "The Little Arabs of the Night," *Collier's*, XXX (March 7, 1903), 11; and "Newsboy Wanderers," *New York Evening Post* (January 24, 1903), p. 1.

2. *The Plague in its Stronghold* (New York, 1903); "The Prayer of the Tenement—The Prayer Unanswered," *Charities*, XII (April 16, 1904), 394-95; "The Lung Block," *Charities*, XI (September 5, 1903), 193.

3. "The Prayer of the Tenement—The Prayer Unanswered," pp. 394-95; "Reform on the Bowery," *World Today*, VIII (January, 1905), 57-62; "From Sweatshop to Factory," *Outlook*, LXXV (November 21, 1903), 688-91; "The Sweating Device Applied to the Home," *Independent*, LVI (April 21, 1904), 898-901.

4. "Dutch and the Skinner," *Everybody's Magazine*, X (February, 1904), 223-29, and "A Slow Man," *Everybody's Magazine*, X (April, 1904), 484-89.

5. "How a Labor Machine Held Up Chicago," *World Today*, VII (July, 1904), 896-905.

6. "The Disappearing Public," *World Today*, VII (August, 1904), 1056-62.

7. "The Stock Yards Strike," *Outlook*, LXXVII (August 13, 1904), 884-89.

8. "The Meat Strike," *Independent*, LVII (July 28, 1904), 179-84; "Packingtown during the Strike," *World Today*, VII (October, 1904), 1271-74.

9. "Packingtown during the Strike," p. 1271; Rose C. Feld, "Mr. Poole Ventures a Glance into the Future," *New York Times Book Review* (February 3, 1924), pp. 2, 26.

10. "Katharine Breshkovsky," *Outlook*, LXXIX (January 7, 1905), 78-88; *Katharine Breshkovsky: "For Russia's Freedom"* (Chicago, 1905).

11. "St. Petersburg Is Quiet," *Outlook*, LXXIX (March 18, 1905), 680-90.

12. Worth reading are "Salvatore Schneider," *Current Literature*, XIX (August, 1908), 176-86; "Haggerty the Lionhearted," *Saturday Evening Post*, CLXXX (June 13, 1908), 6-7, 28-29; "A Man for Ten Years," *Everybody's Magazine*, XXVII (July, 1912), 93-99; "Getting That Home," *Saturday Evening Post*, CLXXIX (July 7, 1906), 7-9, 18.

13. In order to save space in these notes, I have omitted all citations of individual book reviews. They may be located in *Book Review Digest* or in my doctoral dissertation.

14. "The Widening Sense of Honor," *Outlook*, LXXXIV (December 1, 1906), 819-23; "Rebuilding Our Cities," *Saturday Evening Post*, CLXXX (August 10, 1907), 3-4, 30; "Art and Democracy," *Outlook*, LXXXV (March 23, 1907), 665-74; "Chicago's Public Playgrounds," *Outlook*, LXXXVII (December 7, 1907), 775-81.

15. See his forceful and ironic "The People Want to Be Amused," *New York Evening Call* (November 12, 1908), p. 6; (November 14, 1908), p. 6; (November 16, 1908), p. 6.

Chapter Three

1. Walter B. Rideout, *The Radical Novel in the United States* (Cambridge, Massachusetts, 1956), p. 49.

2. John R. Commons, *History of Labor in the United States* (New York, 1935), pp. 265-73.

3. See "The Men on the Docks," *Outlook*, LXXXVI (May 25, 1907), 142-44; "The Ship Must Sail on Time," *Everybody's Magazine*, XIX (August, 1908), 176-86; "The World of Wharves," *Harper's Weekly*, LIV (April 23, 1910), 15-16.

4. Later practices are described in "Ernest Poole," *Wilson Bulletin*, VI (September, 1931), 24. The quotations are from *The Bridge* (New York, 1940), pp. 200-10.

5. Commons, *op cit.*, pp. 274-77.

6. Rideout, *op. cit.*, pp. 34, 54, 63.
7. *Ibid.*, p. 57.
8. Feld, *op. cit.*, pp. 2, 26. According to certain family traditions, several characters in the novel besides the narrator were inspired by real people: Margaret Ann Poole was supposedly the prototype of Eleanore; Bertha Poole Weyl, who had been involved in organizing garment workers, may have been the basis for Sue; and H. G. Wells, whom Poole met during his visit to the United States in 1906, is thought to have been the unnamed English novelist who urges Billy to write a novel.
9. *The Harbor* (New York, 1915), p. 224.
10. Paul Elmer More, "Economic Ideals," *Shelburne Essays, Eleventh Series* (New York, 1921), pp. 235-56; Henry L. Mencken, "A Bad Novelist," *Prejudices, First Series* (New York, 1919), pp. 145-49.
11. Unpublished letter to Arthur B. Maurice, July 17, 1922, Princeton University Library; E. B. Richards, "Introduction," *The Harbor* (New York, 1925), p. xiii.
12. Alice P. Hackett, *Fifty Years of Best Sellers: 1895-1945* (New York, 1945), p. 32. The statistics on sales were provided by the Macmillan Company at the request of Mrs. Poole. The expurgation removed the incident concerning the drunken prostitute and other sexual allusions but preserved such words as "damn."
13. John Dos Passos, *U.S.A.: The Big Money* (New York, 1946), p. 117; John P. Marquand, *H. M. Pulham, Esquire* (Boston, 1941), p. 187.
14. Unpublished letter from Felicia Geffen to T. F. Keefer, August 15, 1959.
15. Louis Filler, *Crusaders for American Liberalism* (New York, 1939), p. 61; John Chamberlain, *Farewell to Reform* (New York, 1933), p. 197; V. L. Parrington, *Main Currents in American Thought* (New York, 1930), p. 350; Rideout, *op. cit.*, p. 56.
16. Rideout, *op. cit.*, pp. 85-86, 286.
17. A. H. Quinn, *American Fiction* (New York, 1936), p. 640; Fred Millett, *Contemporary American Authors* (New York, 1940), p. 78.

Chapter Four

1. "Why I Am No Longer a Pacifist," *McClure's Magazine*, XLIX (August, 1917), 19, 67.
2. See an interview of Poole on his return: "Thinks German Collectivism Will Be Victor," *New York Evening Post* (January 30, 1915), pp. 1, 10.
3. In an unpublished letter to John Reed, dated April 26, 1915

(Harvard University Library), Poole stated that he had now un-snarled his thinking about his new book.

4. A second and most convincing explanation of the origin of three, rather than two, sisters was offered by Otto Tod Mallery, who pointed out that three of Poole's sisters bore amazing resemblances to the fictional heroines. Helen Poole, like Laura, was a very charming person best described as a "social butterfly"; Bertha, who married Walter Weyl, was an intellectual woman like Deborah and, further-more, produced like her only one child; and Alice, who reminds one of Edith, was a maternal woman whose chief interest was her family. Mrs. Ernest Poole, on the other hand, does not accept the idea that the sisters were based on the novelist's relatives.

5. "Visiting Nurses Need Help," *New York Times* (January 11, 1936), p. 14.

6. Hackett, *op. cit.*, p. 34.

7. See *"The Dark People": Russia's Crisis* (New York, 1918), p. 229.

8. "Pulitzer Medal Given to the Times," *New York Times* (June 4, 1918), p. 11.

9. Mencken, *op. cit.*, pp. 145-49. See Poole's view of Mencken in an unpublished letter to Royal Cortissoz, November 30, 1927, Yale University Library.

Chapter Five

1. Harry W. Laidler, *Social-Economic Movements* (New York, 1949), p. 590.

2. "Socialists Here See German Trick," *New York Times* (May 9, 1917), p. 3. Hillquit, Poole's mentor a decade earlier, was denounced in this statement as a pro-German engaged in treasonable activities.

3. George Creel, *How We Advertised America* (New York, 1920), pp. 71, 103.

4. Creel, *op. cit.*, p. 353; "Why I Am No Longer A Pacifist," pp. 19, 67; and "The Fighters and the Haters," *McClure's Magazine*, XLIX (September, 1917), 19.

5. James R. Mock and Cedric Larson, *Words That Won the War* (Princeton, 1939), pp. 72, 241.

6. "Ernest Poole," *World's Work*, XXXIX (March, 1920), 502.

7. *Ibid.*

8. Baldwin, *op. cit.*, pp. 27-28.

9. Frederick Lewis Allen, *Only Yesterday* (New York, 1931), pp. 17-18, 31, 40-41.

10. *Ibid.*, pp. 20-31.

11. In 1922 Poole himself listed *Blind* as his favorite book although he confessed he had read none of his novels since their publication;

he said *Blind* would interest him most and would probably be read more and more widely because of its reception in Europe. See "Ernest Poole, '02," *Princetonian* (February 22, 1922), p. 3. The writing of *Blind* may have been complicated by a false start, if we may regard the statement of the fictional author, Larry Hart, as evidence. Hart says that his first draft idealized the pre-war period in an attempt to show how the war had changed American ways of thought. Determined to tell the truth, he rewrote his novel and gave a realistic picture of the greedy grabbing of the capitalists of the post-Civil War period (*Blind* [New York, 1920], p. 408).

12. Millett, *op. cit.*, p. 527; see also "Ernest Poole and His Work," a draft of a news release apparently written by Poole in 1923, copy in the Duke University Library.

13. Unpublished letter to Arthur B. Maurice.

Chapter Six

1. "The Will to Peace," *New York Times* (November 16, 1921), p. 18; "Is Fascism Dead?" *Outlook*, CXXXIV (July 4, 1923), 316-18; "Rome," *Woman's Home Companion*, L (November, 1923), 23-24.

2. *Blind*, p. 415.

3. *Ibid.*

4. *The Bridge* (New York, 1940), p. 182, describes the public school used for certain scenes in *His Family* and, it appears, as the setting for *Beggars' Gold*. Some of the traits of the principal, a Mr. Doty, may have appeared in the character Peter Wells.

5. For the stories about the clergymen, see the unpublished letter to Arthur B. Maurice. One of them, William L. Stidger, made very effective use of the novel as the basis for one of the sermons in *There Are Sermons in Books* (New York, 1922), pp. 67-82.

6. See Poole's account of his method in "Ernest Poole and His Work."

7. *Blind*, p. 415.

8. E. F. Edgett, "Ernest Poole's Story of a Family," *Boston Evening Transcript* (April 21, 1923), p. 4.

9. The chief source of data is the letter from Ernest Poole to Harold Latham, a Macmillan editor, May 10, 1923, Macmillan Company files. A version of it is found in "Ernest Poole and His Work" and in "Ernest Poole," *Wilson Bulletin*, p. 24. Also important are the letters to William R. Kane, editor of *Editor Magazine*, May 8, 1923, Macmillan Company files, and to Walter Eaton, June 8, 1923, Barrett Collection, University of Virginia.

10. Letter to Latham.

11. Letter to Eaton.

12. Letter to Kane.

13. Poole admitted in his letter to Kane that Miss Tillinghast was based on a real person, but he did not identify her.

14. Letter to Latham.

15. Letter to Eaton.

16. E. E. Hawkins, *United States Catalog Supplement: July, 1921-June, 1924* (New York, 1924), p. 1517; Mary Burnham, *United States Catalog: Books in Print January 1, 1928* (New York, 1928), p. 2259, and *Cumulative Book Index: 1928-1932* (New York, 1933), p. 1645.

17. Feld, *op. cit.*, pp. 2, 26.

18. *Ibid.*

19. "The Avalanche," *Harper's Magazine*, CXLVI (March, 1920), 500-5.

20. Feld, *op. cit.*, p. 26.

21. See the letter to Josephine Piercy.

22. *The Great White Hills of New Hampshire* (New York, 1946), pp. 263, 381.

23. Piercy, *op. cit.*, pp. 537-48.

24. See, for example, Carl Van Doren, *Contemporary American Novelists: 1900-1920* (New York, 1922), p. 136.

25. Unpublished letter from Ernest Poole to Edwin Bjorkman, c. 1922, Pack Memorial Library.

Chapter Seven

1. Unpublished letter to Lillian Wald, October 14, 1926, New York Public Library.

2. *The Great White Hills of New Hampshire*, p. 287.

3. Millett, *op. cit.*, p. 527; "Ernest Poole and His Work," a news release apparently written by Poole in 1930, copy in Duke University Library.

4. Robert E. Spiller, *Literary History of the United States* (New York, 1948), III, 150. See, however, Bessie Graham, *The Bookman's Manual* (New York, 1941), pp. 609-10, where the novel is listed as one of Poole's best-known books. In the 1948 edition the new editor omitted Poole entirely.

5. Letter to Robert W. Anthony published in his *Twenty-Fifth Year Record of the Class of 1902, Princeton University* (Princeton, 1928), p. 243; unpublished letter to Lillian Wald.

6. "The Men at Geneva," *Century*, CXII (September, 1926), 513-25.

7. One of Poole's close friends during the Twenties, for example, was Thomas W. Lamont, head of J. P. Morgan (unpublished letter from William Morris Poole to T. F. Keefer, February 15, 1960).

8. Another possible indication of the success of the novel is its inclusion in summary form in Helen Rex Keller, *The Reader's Digest of Books* (New York, 1936), p. 1331.

9. Upton Sinclair, *Money Writes* (New York, 1927), pp. 117, 205.

10. "Milestones," *Time*, LXXII (October 6, 1958), 86.

11. *Nurses on Horseback* (New York, 1932), p. 107.

12. *The Great White Hills of New Hampshire*, p. 295.

13. Irene and Allen Cleaton, *Books and Battles* (Cambridge, Massachusetts, 1937), pp. 64-65.

14. Feld, *op. cit.*, pp. 2, 26; see the unpublished letters to Zona Gale, March 4 [1928?], Wisconsin State Historical Society; to Hamlin Garland, c. March, 1924, University of Southern California Library; to Harper Brothers, December 9, 1915, Yale University Library; and to Sinclair Lewis, April 12, 1917, Yale University Library.

15. *Nurses on Horseback*, p. 107: "I mean that behind all his [Lewis'] savage attacks lies the cause of 'em. . . . Lewis wants a better world than the one we're living in." Also see *Great Winds* (New York, 1933), pp. 10-11, in which a fictional novelist propounds Poole's views on the kind of readers he wants.

16. In a letter describing *The Destroyer* Poole stressed both the sincerity of the hero of the novel and the fact that he at first did some good work; but, of course, his purely destructive point of view left him at last with the feeling that life was not worth living (unpublished letter to a Mr. Carroll, October 8, 1931, Barrett Collection, University of Virginia).

Chapter Eight

1. "Nurse on Horseback," *Good Housekeeping*, XCIV (June, 1932), 38-39.

2. Unpublished letter from R. L. DeWilton, Macmillan Company, to T. F. Keefer, November 18, 1954.

3. One example is Poole's story "Dream Ships," *Cosmopolitan*, LXXXIII (September, 1927), 76-77 (seemingly an account of an actual event), which tells of a businessman who, driven by overwork to the point of a breakdown, finds physical and spiritual health by taking up sketching ships. Many details from this story are repeated in *Great Winds*.

4. *The Great White Hills of New Hampshire*, pp. 171-72, 177-84.

5. *Ibid.*, pp. 177-83.

6. Unpublished letter from George P. Britt to Poole, January 4, 1936, Macmillan Company files.

7. Unpublished letter to George P. Britt, c. January, 1936, Macmillan Company files.

8. Untitled contribution to the news bulletin of the National Institute, February 1, 1937, National Institute Collection.

9. Untitled contribution to the news bulletin of the National Institute, February 1, 1939, National Institute Collection.

10. Poole also blamed the European War for slowing the sales (unpublished letter to Upton Sinclair, October 1, 1941, Indiana University Library).

Chapter Nine

1. "Topics of the Day," *New York Times* (May 1, 1941), p. 22, and "Ehret Back in U.S. from Italian Jail," *New York Times* (June 3, 1941), p. 11.

2. See John Holmes and Carroll Towle, "Carter Harrison," *A Complete College Reader* (New York, 1950), I, 65-73, and H. V. Procknow, *Great Stories from Great Lives* (New York, 1944), pp. 222-25. The latter reprints three passages from the account of Doctor Frank Billings.

3. Unpublished letter to William Lyon Phelps, February 4, 1943, Yale University Library.

4. Unpublished letter from Howard Cady to T. F. Keefer, April 24, 1959.

5. *Ibid.* In *The Bridge,* however, Poole said in 1940 that several of his acquaintances in New Hampshire urged him to write stories of the life in the area (p. 345); accordingly, the idea may have been in mind for a number of years.

6. *The Great White Hills of New Hampshire,* p. 354, and "Foreword," *The Nancy Flyer* (New York, 1949), pp. vii-ix, give in detail the sources used.

7. In November Mrs. Poole described her husband as too sick to answer mail. See her unpublished letter to the National Institute of Arts and Letters, c. November 20, 1948, National Institute Collection.

8. "Ernest Poole, 69, Novelist, Is Dead," *New York Times* (January 11, 1950), p. 23.

Selected Bibliography

PRIMARY SOURCES

A. *Books*

The Avalanche. New York: Macmillan Company, 1924.

Beggars' Gold. New York: Macmillan Company, 1921.

Blind: A Story of These Times. New York: Macmillan Company, 1920.

The Bridge: My Own Story. New York: Macmillan Company, 1940.

The Car of Croesus. New York: Macmillan Company, 1930.

Danger. New York: Macmillan Company, 1923.

"The Dark People": Russia's Crisis. New York: Macmillan Company, 1918.

The Destroyer. New York: Macmillan Company, 1931.

Giants Gone: The Men Who Made Chicago. New York: McGraw-Hill Company, 1943.

The Great White Hills of New Hampshire. New York: Doubleday, Doran and Company, 1946.

Great Winds. New York: Macmillan Company, 1933.

The Harbor. New York: Macmillan Company, 1915.

His Family. New York: Macmillan Company, 1917.

His Second Wife. New York: Macmillan Company, 1918.

The Hunter's Moon. New York: Macmillan Company, 1925.

The Little Dark Man and other Russian Sketches. New York: Macmillan Company, 1925.

Millions. New York: Macmillan Company, 1922.

The Nancy Flyer: A Stagecoach Epic. New York: Thomas Y. Crowell Company, 1949.

Nurses on Horseback. New York: Macmillan Company, 1932.

One of Us. New York: Macmillan Company, 1934.

Silent Storms. New York: Macmillan Company, 1927.

The Village: Russian Impressions. New York: Macmillan Company, 1918.

The Voice of the Street: A Story of Temptation. New York: Barnes and Company, 1906.

With Eastern Eyes. New York: Macmillan Company, 1926.

B. *Newspaper and Periodical Contributions: Fiction*

"Any Night Is Holy Night When a Child Is Born," *American Magazine*, CIX (January, 1930), 64-65, 144-46.

"Dutch and the Skinner," *Everybody's Magazine*, X (February, 1904), 223-29.

"Edgar Ain't Wuth It," *Collier's*, LXXX (December 10, 1927), 20, 26.

"Getting That Home," *Saturday Evening Post*, CLXXIX (July 7, 1906), 7-9, 18.

"Haggerty the Lionhearted," *Saturday Evening Post*, CLXXX (June 13, 1908), 6-7, 28-29.

"Man for Ten Years," *Everybody's Magazine*, XXVII (July, 1912), 93-99.

"Man Who Loved Two Women," *Cosmopolitan*, LXXX (January, 1926), 88-89.

"One of Us," *Redbook*, LI (July, 1928), 58-61, 103-4.

"Queerest Thing in America," *Saturday Evening Post*, CLXXIX (October 20, 1906), 8-10, 25-27.

"Reform on the Bowery," *World Today*, VIII (January, 1905), 57-62.

"Salvatore Schneider," *Current Literature*, XIX (August, 1908), 176-86.

"Shadow of the Sword," *Redbook*, LXXII (November, 1938), 16-19, 82-85.

"Slow Man," *Everybody's Magazine*, X (April, 1904), 484-89.

"Up from the Ghetto," *Saturday Evening Post*, CLXXVIII (March 17, 1906), 8-9, 18.

C. *Other Newspaper and Periodical Contributions (excluding those cited in notes):*

"Abraham Cahan," *Outlook*, XCIX (October 28, 1911), 467-78.

"Berlin," *Saturday Evening Post*, CLXXXVII (April 17, 1915), 20-22, 77-79.

"Blind Revolutionist," *Everybody's Magazine*, XXII (January, 1910), 3-12.

"Brandeis," *American Magazine*, LXXI (February, 1911), 481-93. Enlarged as foreword in Louis B. Brandeis, *Business—A Profession* (Boston: Small, Maynard, and Company, 1914 and 1933).

"City's Dream of a City," *Everybody's Magazine*, XXIII (July, 1910), 1-13.

"Convention of the Zealous," *Collier's*, XLI (June 13, 1908), 9-10.

"Dounya," *Independent*, LIX (October 26, 1905), 974-80.

"Face of My Enemy," *Everybody's Magazine*, XXXII (May, 1915), 529-42.

Selected Bibliography

"Harnessing Socialism," *American Magazine*, LXVI (September, 1908), 427-32.

"Human 'Submarines' in the Zone of European War," *Current Opinion*, LVIII (June, 1915), 435-36.

"Jewish Girl's Struggle to Rise in Russia," *Outlook*, LXXXII (January 20, 1906), 125-31.

"Men Who Are to Vote," *Everybody's Magazine*, XV (October, 1906), 435-44.

"Prussian Monument," *New Republic*, V (December 4, 1915), 114-16.

"Russia's Bastille," *Saturday Evening Post*, CLXXVIII (May 12, 1906), 6-7, 24-25.

"Russian Hamlet," *Outlook*, LXXIX (April 29, 1905), 1035-40.

"Russian Villager," *Outlook*, LXXX (May 13, 1905), 113-18.

"Small Town Sees the World," *World Today*, VII (September, 1904), 1143-49.

"Theatre of War," *American Magazine*, LXXIX (June, 1915), 28-30, 62, 64, 66, 68-71.

"Till Russia Shall Be Free," *Saturday Evening Post*, CLXXVIII (April 7, 1906), 1-2, 26-27.

"Underground Fire in Russia," *Saturday Evening Post*, CLXXVIII (April 21, 1906), 1-3, 22-24.

"With the Caucasian Revolutionists," *Outlook*, LXXXI (November 18, 1905), 653-61.

SECONDARY SOURCES

No extended studies of Poole have previously been published and hardly any competent criticism. Most of the comment on his works is located in book reviews (see the list in my dissertation or in Book Review Digest).

ANTHONY, ROBERT WARREN. "Ernest Poole." *Twenty-Fifth Year Record of the Class of 1902, Princeton University*. Princeton, c. 1928, 149-50. Includes Poole's own account of his literary career in a letter to the editor.

BALDWIN, CHARLES C. *The Men Who Make Our Novels*. New York: Dodd, Mead, and Company, 1919. Contains biographical details not available elsewhere.

"Ernest Poole." *Wilson Bulletin*, VI (September, 1931), 24. Biographical detail including the background of *Danger*.

"Ernest Poole, '02." *Princetonian* (February 22, 1922), pp. 1, 3. Biographical detail, some drawn from interviews.

FELD, ROSE C. "Mr. Poole Ventures a Glance into the Future." *New York Times Book Review* (February 3, 1924), pp. 2, 26. The only published extended interview with Poole about his literary ideas.

MENCKEN, HENRY L. *Prejudices, First Series.* New York: Alfred A. Knopf, Inc., 1919. The attack that Poole never forgave.

MILLETT, FRED B. *Contemporary American Authors.* New York: Harcourt, Brace, and Company, 1940. Short biography and bibliography.

MORE, PAUL ELMER. "Economic Ideals." *Shelburne Essays, Eleventh Series.* New York: Houghton-Mifflin Company, 1921. An attack by a humanist on the materialistic values of Poole the socialist.

PIERCY, JOSEPHINE K. *Modern Writers at Work.* New York: Macmillan Company, 1930. Contains a letter from Poole about his work.

PARRINGTON, VERNON L. *Main Currents in American Thought.* New York: Harcourt, Brace, and Company, 1930. Describes Poole as potential naturalist destroyed by reform movement.

QUINN, ARTHUR H. *American Fiction.* New York: Appleton-Century Company, 1936. Unbiased literary criticism—all four pages of it.

RICHARDS, EDWIN B. "Introduction," *The Harbor.* New York: Macmillan Company, 1925. A competent discussion by the editor of the high school edition.

RIDEOUT, WALTER B. *The Radical Novel in the United States.* Cambridge, Massachusetts: Harvard University Press, 1956. An objective and accurate analysis of Poole's political position in *The Harbor.*

VAN DOREN, CARL. *Contemporary American Novelists: 1900-1920.* New York: Macmillan Company, 1922. Asserted that Poole's "magic" had departed.

WARFEL, HARRY. *American Novelists of Today.* New York: American Book Company, 1951. Short bibliography, plot summaries, brief commentary.

Index

Index